A DOG BESIDE ME:

Recollections of a Shooting Man

A DOG BESIDE ME
Recollections of a Shooting Man

ARTHUR CADMAN, OBE

Foreword by
Major-General David Lloyd Owen,
CB, DSO, OBE, MC

Illustrated by
John Tickner

• THE •
SPORTSMAN'S
PRESS
LONDON

Published by The Sportsman's Press 1993

©Arthur Cadman 1993

To PHYL
Who shared so many of the lives of my early dogs

A catalogue record for this book
is available from the British Library

ISBN 0–948253–63–0

Printed in Great Britain by Redwood Books

CONTENTS

AUTHOR'S NOTE

I would like to express my thanks to Mrs M. J. Cadman for typing my difficult drafts and for other help.

A.C.

FOREWORD

by Major-General David Lloyd Owen, CB, DSO, OBE, MC

HAVING known, and admired, Arthur Cadman as a great naturalist and lover of country sports for close on twenty years, I have been looking forward to this book. All the more so because I have also been lucky enough to have known many of the dogs which feature in it as his companions.

I know of few people with such a complete harmony with their dogs as Arthur Cadman; and this little book is full of delightful anecdotes about those that have made such an important contribution to his life. It is quite brilliantly illustrated by John Tickner's inimitable sketches.

Perhaps I was a little surprised by Arthur's apparent sensitivity when he relates how he did not wish to subject his host's brand new car to having to carry his extremely muddy and enormous labrador between drives at a pheasant shoot just after the last war. I remember so well another devoted lover of dogs coming to see me in Norfolk a few years ago in his immaculate, new Volvo saloon car. On the back seat were his beloved, and slightly unruly, labrador and springer spaniel. Both were wet and quite muddy.

When I asked this friend if he hadn't got a rug or something for his dogs to sit on, he replied, 'Well, it's not their fault I've got a new car.'

Arthur Cadman's book has similar tales about his dogs which have meant so much to him.

INTRODUCTION

E VER since the first wolf dog crept into the first Cave Man's cave and curled up in front of his log fire, man, especially Hunting man, has been dependant upon his canine companions. First, the dogs learnt to assist man in his hunting of wild creatures for food for the whole family. Gradually over the years, man trained his dogs for specialist work in relation to this daily need to obtain meat for food. Later, dogs became guards for the cave man's family and children. When most of the different requirements had been met, the dog became a household pet, to act as the constant companion of the very young and the very old.

There is no doubt at all that the closest rapport between man and dog

'. . . the dog became a household pet'

developed when hunting was the prime need. So it is today. Dogs which share field sports with their owners become more close to them, and develop more intimate relationships than the fat little town dog pets can do to their owners.

The instinct to hunt is in the make-up of every dog, even though the one human being, who shares his life, may have no interest in the great country sports and pastimes of the British countryside.

People whose dogs share their sport find that their own pleasure in the different sports which they follow is immensely enhanced by the helpful participation of their dog. This is true, especially, in all forms of shooting.

In many places the bird dog will find and indicate the precise position of the quarry. Thus, pointers and setters will range the open moor and stand 'on point' when they wind the game hidden in the heather. But it is not their job to retrieve the birds that are shot. This is the normal task of the various breeds of retrieving dog. The wildfowler, whose sport is very often near to water, needs a dog to swim for and retrieve the geese or ducks which he shoots. It takes a strong dog to catch up and retrieve a wounded goose on a fast flowing river, or out on the flowing tide.

Other dogs, spaniels especially, are used for flushing game out of dense cover. They must face brambles and gorse and be prepared to hunt woodcock or pheasant.

Some of the early breeds, wolf hounds and deer hounds, are no longer used in the shooting field. But that does not mean that a stalker, particularly a man who stalks deer in woodland, does not need a dog to assist him. Most breeds, and even mongrels, may be trained to accompany a stalker when he stalks deer. All dogs have attributes which man has lost, long ago, during the process of so-called civilisation. A dog's hearing is much more acute than a man's. And man's nose is grossly inferior to any dog's nose, since a dog's ability to scent the quarry is surprisingly efficient. A dog can wind a deer over 200 metres away and thus indicate to his master exactly where that deer is located, even in dense cover. Should the stalker have the misfortune to wound a deer, his dog should be able to locate it and assist in its final recovery.

Other dogs used for country pursuits are foxhounds, staghounds, beagles and greyhounds. Many poachers use lurchers and other forms of greyhounds for catching hares and other game, illegally.

Of course, sheepdogs and cattle dogs are used for farming practices, which end in food for man.

It is a fact that all dogs used for country pursuits enjoy their job immensely. A gun dog knows, always, when his master is going out shooting, because of the scent of gun oil on his master's hands. His excitement is plain for all to see!

Choosing the breed which one wishes to have is not always easy. Choosing a name for a new puppy is often difficult too, although many a puppy's name just arrives, based on some trait that the puppy develops. There is one name used universally more than any other, both for town dogs and in the shooting field: 'Cwm 'ere'. Usually it denotes a dog which is wont to do anything but obey. In the shooting field, the man who bellows his dog's name on every possible occasion, usually advertises the fact that his dog is disobedient! An unruly dog and a loud-mouthed owner, between them, do much to lessen the day's sport and to conserve the game which both want to see in the bag!

When choosing a suitable name for a dog, it is normal to take note of some of the dog's forebears, as recorded in the pedigree. Many dogs' names represent aspects of sport: Grouse, Teal, Wigeon, Snipe or Snipey, Brent, Mark, Shot, Bullet and so on, even Eley, Purdey or Aya all come within this category. Sheepdogs are often called Shep or Tag; good names for Scottish dogs are Haggis, Jock, Angus, Loch, or Laird.

I have known an occasional Heather and Bracken, whilst there are many yellow labradors and golden retrievers called Honey. Silver, Copper or Sooty are also based on colour. Incidentally these two breeds are sometimes misnamed. Golden labrador or yellow retriever are incorrect and the use of such names gives offence to the owner, just as foxhounds must never be called dogs, although the dog pack, or the bitches, may hunt on separate days.

A dog's name should be short, although in the field it is desirable that the dog should respond to a whistle rather than to his name. In any case, a puppy which is given a name early in his career, often gains a pet name before he is mature. Wog, which was the name of the best dog that I ever had, and Nigger – another wonderful wildfowl dog of mine – are no longer acceptable today. Bear and Mole are good names for black dogs, as is Seal: many a labrador's head looks like a seal when swimming! My Bear was the best goose dog that I have ever known. In his last season he retrieved over 100 geese and only lost one, which went through ice, where he could not follow. Mole was an outstanding deer dog, whose exploits were numerous and whose fame was known to many visiting Continental stalkers.

'Dogs which are named after wives or children may cause confusion'

Some dogs' names follow the bottle. I have known two lovely spaniels, Whisky and Soda, and I had a good yellow labrador called Gin. Brandy for a dog, rather than a bitch, easily becomes Randy. Dogs which are named after wives or children may cause confusion and a Welsh springer, named Jones, was apt to cause much bemusement in Wales.

Sometimes dogs are named after famous people. I have known two outstanding dogs called Cassius and one called Churchill. Although I have known several Maggies, I have never met a four-legged Thatcher, but there are several Majors in the shooting field, and I knew a good deer dog called Fergie, although that was before Prince Andrew was married. Queen and Queenie are not unusual. Rufus is another dog's name, of ancient royal lineage. Monty is a good name for a terrier, as are Vic for Victoria and Nip, for obvious reasons for terriers.

The names of hounds are often much longer than those of shooting dogs. Frequently all of a litter become named with words starting with the same

12

letter. Thus Daffodil, Dainty, Duchess, Duty etc. I have yet to meet a Madonna or even a Monroe in the Field sports world.

My delightful young yellow labrador was called Happy when she was a puppy. No name has ever proved to be so apt. She is happy the day long, perhaps especially so when she does what she 'didn't ought' to do! Puppies and especially labradors, are happy by nature and shooting dogs lead very happy lives. So my Happy is the best named dog that I know.

I have had a dog, Friday, and a Mischief, both lovely dogs which met with mishaps before they became mature, and also a Biscuit.

But, above all else, it is the whistle and obedience thereto which is all important in the shooting field.

I

DIFFERENT GUNDOG BREEDS

THERE are many different breeds of gundog, each bred for its specialised duties. Broadly the work of gundogs may be divided into those that are required to find game and those whose duty it is to retrieve game after it has been shot. The stalking man's dog is another requirement.

Dogs bred for generations with the object of finding game are pointers, setters and spaniels. Pointers were first introduced to this country in the eighteenth century from Spain where, before the days of shooting birds on the wing, partridges were netted after being located by the pointer. These early pointers were crossed with foxhounds to give stamina and greater pace. But a pointer should work with his head held high to catch wind scent; a foxhound follows the ground scent with his nose close to the ground.

The early pointers were used primarily for partridges. Their scenting powers were second to none. Selective breeding was required to breed out the lower-held noses of the foxhound influence. Pointers (and setters) were used for finding birds for falconry. Shooting over bird dogs was suited to the slow rate of fire of muzzle loaders and flintlock guns. This method of shooting became a very useful way of making a bag of grouse before the invention of the breech-loader, which resulted in the popularity of driven game shooting.

Normally only two guns shoot over bird dogs. A second gun may be carried by a gamekeeper to replace the gun that has been fired (if a muzzle loader) and the dog handler works the bird dogs, usually run as a couple. The dogs are worked into the wind, or sometimes across the wind, and they cover a much greater area of ground than could be worked by the guns walking alone. When the dog finds game it comes to point, the second dog backing it as soon as it sees the point. The two guns move to the point, one on either side, and the handler then urges the dog on point to advance slowly, until the bird, or birds, flush. After the shot, it is not normal for the

An early pointer

bird dog to retrieve, although some pointers and setters have become adept at retrieving. This job should be done by a retrieving dog kept in abeyance behind the line.

Besides pointers, the three breeds of setters were used as game dogs – Irish, English and the Gordon setter. In Ireland, where perhaps game was less numerous than in Scotland, nearly all shooting was done over setters, and in America bird dogs were used chiefly for quail shooting.

It was the advent of driven shooting on an ever increasing scale that led to the decline of shooting over dogs and to the great increase of the use of retrieving dogs. But grouse shooting over pointers or setters is still carried out in Ross-shire and on moorland where the stock of grouse is insufficient for driving.

Shooting over pointers or setters is a great sport. The dog work is fascinating to watch and the excitement of approaching a dog on point, knowing that the quarry may explode at any moment, is intense. On the other hand shooting over dogs, or other forms of walking up grouse in line, is not so good for the future of the moor; in driving a higher proportion of

15

old cocks and barren pairs is shot but when walking up, the young birds provide the easiest shots.

Pointing dogs may be used effectively for ptarmigan. But a pointer that ranges wide and fast is at risk, as ptarmigan often inhabit rocky or stoney ground, where a fast dog may have a nasty injury, usually to the shoulder. It is a long way to get an injured dog (or man!) from ptarmigan ground back to the car.

In modern times, the introduction of the German pointer and the Hungarian vizsla, has given the one-dog man a chance to have an all-purpose dog, suitable for retrieving too. The vizsla is a beautiful breed, although its relatively thin coat makes it less suitable for retrieving wildfowl than many other breeds. These two breeds are known as HPRs ('Hunt point retriever dogs'). The Brittany spaniel introduced in 1982, also comes under this heading and it is a very attractive air-scenting dog, much to be recommended. They have naturally short (as if docked) tails.

German pointers, which became popular after World War II, may be short-haired or wire-haired. They are good in water and also make excellent dogs for deer stalkers. Another breed, the Weimaraner, is often used and this breed is popular in America. These dogs and the German pointers are strong, large dogs with great stamina. They tend to be one-man dogs, only really obedient to their owner, and some say they are rather aloof.

The German Munsterlander, introduced in 1972, is another useful HPR breed. They are black and white or sometimes mottled roan, and very keen,yet biddable. Also from Germany comes the Wachtel; this name literally means 'quail dog'.

The Italian spinone, another HPR, is not often seen in the British shooting field. They have a very nice temperament, but tend to be slow workers.

Except for basic discipline all bird dogs require specialised training, which is usually beyond the amateur dog owner. The HPRs tend to range much more widely than do English pointers and the setters. They are very intelligent dogs, hence the need for very intelligent handling when training!

The various breeds of spaniels are used for finding and flushing game in cover, and retrieving. Normally they do not point. The main breeds are the English springer, the Welsh springer, the clumber and the cocker. The cocker is a very small breed and it is questionable if it is suitable for carrying heavy game such as cock pheasants, hares and geese.

The job of the spaniel is to 'spring' game and they must, and do work the thickest cover of brambles, gorse etc. It is normal for spaniels' tails to be docked and most sportsmen agree that this is essential. An undocked spaniel grows a feathery tail which collects burrs, thorns and grass seeds. As the tail is wagging all the time the dog is working, the undocked tail may become torn and bleeding and can take a long time to heal.

Training, and especially keeping a spaniel under tight control, is not as easy as, say, training a labrador. They are fine sporting dogs and take to wildfowling well, particularly the Irish water spaniel.

Once I managed a famous goose shoot. One of the regular guns purchased a beautiful Field Trial trained springer spaniel. The first morning flight after he had acquired this dog, the owner was in one of three butts on a peninsula. These butts were cut off by a narrow but deep burn. I was picking up with Honey on the far side of the burn.

Honey was a very good game finder and soon she had a pile of geese at my feet. When the flight was over, I sent her far out after a distant goose. Shortly after I heard the owner of the spaniel exhorting the dog to cross the burn. The dog turned up at my feet and seized one of Honey's dead geese. A moment later I heard: 'What a good dog! He's got a goose!' Then, a few

'The dog turned up at my feet seized one of Honey's dead geese'

moments later, after the dog had repeated the exercise, I heard 'Oh! he's got another! What a good dog!' Soon my pile of geese had all gone. The nearest bridge was half a mile up stream and the guns on the peninsula could only get off by a tricky wade within a couple of inches of the top of their thigh boots. The owner of the Field Trial spaniel had to carry all the geese which, otherwise, I would have carried over relatively easy ground.

Rough shooting over a well-trained, experienced spaniel is always a delight. The first dog I ever had was a cross between a clumber and a springer spaniel, which my father gave me when I was eighteen. He looked like a cross between a terrier and a pointer! But that dog, loved companion of so many early shooting exploits, was immensely wise. He taught me more about dogs (and quarry species, too) than I could ever have learnt from a dog training manual. In common with so many wise shooting dogs he would always go round to the far side of a bush in which he knew a pheasant, or rabbit, was lurking in order to flush the game towards me.

When it came to 'hunting' rough ground together, we were a pretty ruthless combination. How well I remember the day he tore his stomach open on a sharp stake. I could see his entrails. In tears I carried him all the way back to my car and took him straight to the nearest vet, a stranger.

I rushed into his surgery and demanded that the vet should stitch up the wound at once. He said: 'If I stitch him up there may be some impurity which will go septic.' (This was before the days of antibiotics). He bathed the wound and told me to take the dog home, put him on a bed of clean straw and pour a drop of olive oil into the wound. 'A dog's tongue is the best possible healing agent,' he said.

I carried out his instructions, thinking the poor dog's days were over. That wound healed a little more each day. The dog hardly moved from his bed of straw. In ten days dear old Noble was back to normal with a cleanly healed scar. We had many days of happy hunting together after that!

Most of the other breeds of shooting dogs come under the retrieving category. First amongst these is my favourite breed, the labrador. Labradors may be black or yellow (never 'golden', which term relates to golden retrievers, a totally different breed) or chocolate. If a yellow bitch is mated to a black dog, or vice versa, the litter will be of mixed colours, either black or yellow, but never skewbald.

The labrador is a real family dog with a lovely temperament which will put up with the teasing hands of children. He is keen to please and is faithful by nature. The retrieving instinct is so bred into a labrador that even the smallest puppy will seek to pick up and carry from the earliest age. Alas, his favourite tit-bit, which he thinks his master will long to have, is not always attractive – a dead rat or long dead baby chick are not the most desired morsels for a human. Therein lies the danger of spoiling the retrieving instinct. Such gifts must be accepted as rare jewels! They must be disposed of out of sight and scent of the puppy – or they will reappear very soon.

A labrador is a very versatile shooting dog. He must learn to retrieve from the thickest cover or the roughest water. When he is experienced he may be used, like a spaniel, to put up game from thick cover, but this is not his main job.

What a lovely sight it is to see a young labrador retrieving his first goose! What enormous pleasure his early successes give to both dog and man! I admit that I am thoroughly biased in favour of the labrador over all other breeds, and labradors by nature are excellent water dogs.

The Newfoundland and Chesapeake Bay breeds are both fantastic wild-fowl dogs. Both tend to be one-owner dogs that will take no notice of anyone else. Flat coat retrievers and golden retrievers are very attractive breeds, both good in water. As house dogs, goldens are rather hairy; especially when coated with mud, they may not be welcome indoors. Curly coated retrievers tend to be somewhat obstinate and maybe they become hard mouthed more frequently than other breeds.

All retrieving dogs must be trained to sit steadily at a peg during a pheasant shoot, or in a grouse butt, or duck hide. The fact that a wildfowl dog may be required to go quickly to recover a wounded goose or duck, tends to result in unsteadiness at a formal driven shoot.

A tip which will make a rather wild dog appear to be as good as gold at the peg of his master, is to put one paw through his collar. That will make him lie flat, usually. Or, of course, there are those dog pegs made in the shape of a giant corkscrew. Sometimes, however, it is difficult to screw them into hard ground.

We have all seen the alternative – of attaching the dog to a cartridge bag. A hare runs past, and cartridges are distributed out of the flapping bag over the countryside, far and wide, much to the amusement of the hare, the other guests and all the beaters!

Other breeds of dogs, not meant for the shooting field, sometimes appear. A sheepdog has immense intelligence and a sheepdog × labrador cross may make a superb gun dog. I knew two daschunds which worked every inch of cover better than any other dog, but perhaps they were too efficient at plucking a dead pheasant. Many years ago I came across a fox terrier called Jack. When all the blue-blooded retrievers had failed on a runner, that little terrier would be put on the line. He *never* failed!

Alsatians too, being super intelligent, sometimes make good rough shooting dogs, but any game that is shot tends to be oven ready by the time it is brought to hand!

The perils of attaching a dog to a cartridge bag

II

DOGS IN THE
SHOOTING FIELD

IT is both human and canine nature that everyone's dog is the Best Ever
and one that can do no wrong – until that hare runs past. Nevertheless
no-one who is a guest gun should take a dog to a shoot without being
invited to do so. It may be embarrassing for the host when a guest says: 'Shall
I bring my dog?' 'What is he?' 'Oh he's a crossbred labrador/sheepdog.' 'Is
he steady?' 'Oh yes. I keep him on the lead.' The host has enough informa-
tion. 'Well, we'll have rather a lot of dogs tomorrow. Perhaps it will be best
if you do not bring yours.'

There is the story of the American visitor who was invited to a week's
grouse driving. He hired a fine looking black labrador from a well-known
kennels. On the morning of the first day, the first shot went off at the far end
of the line. With a delighted bark, the labrador took off and raced up and
down the line of butts causing mayhem. So it was at each drive. At the end
of the day the American sought out the head keeper. 'I'm awfully sorry
about that Brute. What can I do? I have him for the whole week!' 'Don't
worry sir. Tonight I'll load a couple of cartridges with wheat. When he goes
off, give him one up the backside. That will stop him in his tracks.'

The next day the keeper slipped the two wheat cartridges to the American. At the first shot, off went the dog and off went two rounds of wheat.
The dog yelped with surprise and ran faster than ever! As the dog passed the
next butt, in which was a Frenchman, the Frenchman put up his gun and
bowled over the dog, stone dead! He then turned to the American and
beaming with delight shouted: 'How you say? I wipe your eye, eh?'

A wild dog is an embarrassment, especially to its owner and to the captain
of the shoot. 'Take that bloody dog back and shut it up in your car' is a
justified command. Or, at lunch time: 'John, I think your dog is overtired.
Better leave him in the car this afternoon.' In both cases this suggestion is

21

accompanied by the secret wish that the dog will demolish the inside of the car before the owner returns!

Some wild dogs have the luck of the devil. A partridge is dropped into a field of kale that is known to be full of birds and the next beat to be worked. Away goes a huge black and white springer and, by immense good luck, goes straight to the bird (which, also by good fortune, is not a runner) and returns with it almost before its master has started to swear.

We have all seen the other extreme – a very fast, young labrador tearing off wildly to retrieve that partridge. The owner, purple in the face, is blowing a police whistle and the progress of the dog is marked by pheasant after pheasant flushing right down to the boundary of the field of roots.

What few of us have seen in recent years is a grey partridge, shot or alive! How often in those lovely days of long age, the gun who had shot a partridge often thought he knew better than his dog. He would mill round

'The owner, purple in the face, is blowing a police whistle . . .'

and round in the mangles (now as rare as partridges!) whilst his dog followed the runner one hundred yards away.

A wild, uncontrolled and disobedient dog is a menace at any shoot and especially so on the shore. Such a dog spoils everyone's sport. Just occasionally the activities of such a dog may be put to good use. At morning flight I have known geese to settle far away in the wrong place. But someone's unruly dog has also seen them and goes tearing off, putting up the geese which, by good fortune, give someone a shot.

No-one should leave a dog in the back of a vehicle with dead game, at the end of the day. That is asking for trouble. Many seasons ago a great friend of mine shot his first pinkfoot. 'Arthur, I'll have that goose's head mounted,' he said. We were only twenty minutes away from his house, but when we got out of the car, his big black labrador was grinning from ear to ear, that goose's head safely in his belly.

On another occasion I saw the only quail shot that I have ever seen shot. Our host decided to have it stuffed. At lunch time all that remained was a leg and a few feathers – and several guilty looking dogs in the back of his Land Rover!

Game should be hung, as soon as possible, out of reach of dogs, preferably in the game vehicle. One man should be in charge of that job; he should hang young birds separately from old. Binder twine, cut into suitable lengths beforehand, eases his task.

All game should be hung by the neck, with the feathers smoothed, in a cool place secure from bluebottles. A fly spray applied to the head will tend to keep them away.

Every sportsman should treat the game that he has shot with respect. There is pleasure in smoothing the feathers and perhaps noting some abnormality in the plumage. At a duck shoot identifying the different species, and sexes, and even the different stages of the plumage of the young is always of interest. At the end of the day the owner may say: 'Would you like a brace of pheasants or a couple of duck?' He who prefers the duck can tell young from old by the shape of the end of the tail feathers. The old have pointed ends, but young have a sort of W at the end, although by November young birds may have moulted to grow adult-shaped tail feathers. Often, with geese, this difference is important.

Incidentally the misuse of the ancient word 'brace' is all too common nowadays. Brace (or leash) applies to game birds, although at the end of the day the bag of pheasants is marked by the total number – 130 birds, not 65 brace, Rabbits, hares, duck, geese and all species other than game birds should be called 'couples', not 'brace'. The expression 'a brace of rabbits' (or duck etc.,) is a term which grates on the ears of a true sportsman.

In the hunting field it is permissable to refer to a brace, or leash of foxes. But hounds are counted in couples. As with shooting dogs and their masters, so a close rapport develops between 'the Master' and his hounds.

The owner of a certain estate where I used to shoot as a guest, was also Master of the local pack of hounds. But he developed a heart condition, and had to give up hunting them. Some years later hounds met at the hall. They moved across the park to draw the first covert. The ex-Master was riding his old horse, well away from the route taken by the hounds. Suddenly he keeled over and fell off his horse, the result of the heart attack which all his friends had feared. One of the hounds, who were all out of sight of his tragic end, had been his special favourite. That hound knew. He left the pack and ran across the park and stood guard over his old Master's dead body.

There is no doubt that many dogs have psychic attributes. When I was a young lad, aged about seven, my father was training a black cocker spaniel puppy. The training took place on a grass tennis court, the young dog being trained to fetch a dummy to my father, who was standing at one end of the court. All went well for several retrieves. Then, unexpectedly, the young dog picked the dummy and ran to an oak seat on a terrace at the side of the court and stood with his head up, holding the dummy, whilst his tail wagged wildly. It seemed obvious that he was trying to deliver the dummy to someone sitting on the seat. But there was no-one to be seen sitting thereon, nor had any of us been near the seat, so he was not following the scent of anyone who had been to the seat. Everyone who witnessed this incident was convinced that the dog could see someone, or something, that was invisible to us!

There is much difference between what is required of a dog during a day's rough shooting, a driving day or an outing after ducks or pigeons. When shooting ducks and pigeons, the dog's master is usually in a hide. The dog must stay still throughout the time that the master is waiting, and must be out of sight. How often the dog will squirm through the bottom of the hide and become obvious to the approaching ducks, or pigeons. After a successful shot, an uncontrolled dog may dash out taking half the hide with him. Beware a rather wild dog that remains extra quiet. He may be consuming his master's sandwiches.

A dog that dashes out and mistakes decoys for the shot bird is a dreadful

'Beware the rather wild dog that remains extra quiet'

nuisance, especially if he returns festooned with the cords attached to duck decoys! And a dog that retrieves a wounded bird and puts it down before delivering it to hand is also an unmitigated nuisance.

On a driven day a dog must not leave his master's peg or butt until the drive is over. On a grouse moor it is often the bird which has fallen closest to the butt which is overlooked and not picked; all birds after they have been picked should be left on top of the butt or by the peg for collecting by whoever has been given the task of carrying them back.

I remember a grouse day when there were some Italian guns present. At the end of the day, these guests wanted old birds (I think for taxidermy). They cut a short length of bramble and with great dexterity extracted all the guts through the anus! Beaters' and keepers' faces were a picture of astonishment as they watched this version of the gralloch!

It used to be an inviolable tradition to draw the legs of a woodcock as soon as it was retrieved, because woodcock legs are great delicacies. This custom is now but rarely performed, and one sees woodcock hanging in the game larder with their legs intact. Indeed if one is seen drawing a cock's legs after shooting it, one is regarded much as those Italians mentioned above.

The rough shooter's dog is often under much less perfect control than is a retriever sitting at the peg. The rough shooter's dog flushes the bird and, often, he is almost under the bird with his mouth open when it falls dead.

When the wildfowler shoots duck or goose and it falls in water, often he needs the dog to go for it as quickly as possible. Any delay helps a wounded duck to escape. When a goose is shot and falls apparently dead, it must be watched. Many recover and make off quickly. Sometimes a wounded goose will walk about, apparently unconcerned. But they can run as fast as a cock pheasant and they are cunning at hiding themselves, although usually they leave a good scent.

Most experienced dogs learn to observe, and to watch a wounded bird. I remember a splendid pheasant day at which I was a guest. My host had a fine old yellow labrador. This dog sat as good as gold with pheasants falling all around him. But if there was a wounded bird, he would slide away unobtrusively and seek it out at once.

A wildfowl dog that does the same with ducks is invaluable. If tide or river are swirling away a dead duck, the sooner the dog gets after it the better.

On a river where a flight is likely to produce a useful bag falling into the river, it is a good plan to have a picker-up, with a good water dog, stationed some way downstream. Sometimes a net stretched across will serve the same purpose. Wasted game is unacceptable.

Dogs sometimes do irrational things. A dog may swim a river and find a duck on the far side. Nothing is more infuriating if the dog puts down the duck on top of the bank and swims back without it! Another very annoying fault, which is difficult to cure, is the dog that races to another dog already retrieving a bird. In the ensuing tug of war the culinary attributes of the bird are not improved. The best cure is to let the offending dog try this with a jealous, bad-tempered dog or bitch, who will see him off in no uncertain manner. Many dogs become possessive and jealous over game which has been shot and retrieved, and that can start a fight.

Dogs at a picnic lunch can be a nuisance. At such a time one's dog should be put into one's car, or made to sit well away from the food, or tied up, if the dog is not fully trustworthy. Once on a grouse moor, the wife of one of the guns had just put down her husband's sandwiches. A roaming dog came up and cocked his leg over them. When the husband came to eat his lunch, everyone watched with bated breath. The result was totally unexpected. Turning to his wife he asked; 'What have you put into these sandwiches? They are *very* tasty!'

On a moor (and elsewhere) every dog must be totally safe with sheep. When a dog's hunting instincts are aroused, and sheep go belting past, there is a temptation to chase. Such an incident will ensure that neither dog, nor master, is invited to the next shoot!

Dogs that jump up against the doors of vehicles, leaving paw marks and

26

scratches, are most unpopular too. Curiously enough it is usually the most expensive and highly polished vehicle which is chosen by the dog for this treatment – often owned by the horrified host.

As against these stories of bad behaviour, it is a happy master who, at the end of the day, receives praise for his dog's good performance during the day. 'That was a wonderful retrieve after the last drive!' makes up for all the easy misses which may have happened, when one's cartridges have been full of dust!

It is a fact that a gun with a good working and reliable dog will get far more shooting invites than his neighbour with an uncontrolled, unruly brute. Perhaps worst of all is a fighting dog that causes mayhem whenever he meets another male dog. A fight anywhere is abhorrent, but in the back of a Land Rover it can cause a real problem. This is a fault that is difficult to cure, as is a dog that whines. Sooty, a lovely black labrador that I owned, had this fault. At a pheasant shoot I tried putting a stocking over his face, like a bank robber (the idea was to stop him seeing birds falling around him). But it did not work. I heard that an empty Fairy liquid container, or something similar, filled with water and squirted between his eyes, would be a successful deterrent. But who can shoot well with such a weapon in one hand, and a gun in the other?

Sooty was a great wildfowl and deer dog. Although he was such a coward that, if I threatened him with a straw, he would yelp as if being beaten with a stick. He was fearless with a wounded deer, which he would seize by the throat, and hold until I could deal with the situation. But when he whined at a formal shoot, everyone was aware of him.

III

INTELLIGENCE

SOME folk maintain that a dog has no ability to think. That is, he is unable to act upon constructive thought. Of course, sometimes it is difficult to decide whether his actions are due to inborn instinct, or to careful training, both of which may give the impression of careful thought. An elephant never forgets, and dogs, too, have long memories, especially for people, and for other dogs, particularly those bad-tempered enough to have provoked a near fight!

Before World War II I used to follow the river Dovey to a favourite place for a flight. At one point there was a stile, awkward for my dog to get over. The fence at the side of the stile was also difficult, but fifteen yards short of the stile was a hole in the fence, which my dog found and used regularly.

During the war we were both elsewhere. Then came the day when I was able to return to this favourite haunt. The Wog and I proceeded, as before, in the pre-dawn dark. The stile and fence were still there. The dog went straight to the hole in the fence, as if we had used it yesterday. That was memory. A less intelligent dog would have run up and down that fence looking for a weak place to get through, or over.

This fine dog was the best dog I have ever been privileged to own. He and I were very close companions and his exploits are legion. He knew more about shooting than did many post-war guns.

Once I was crouching, with my dog, in a hole at the edge of the saltings. There was a full gale blowing combined with the highest Spring tide. The river, turbulent and wild, raced past. The tide began to spill into my hole. At that moment two wigeon came past, fighting against the gale. I dropped them to a right and left, the first falling 20 yards out and the second 35 to 40 yards away, and the tide whipped them away like two corks.

The old dog slipped into the water as smoothly as an otter. I thought that he would get the nearer duck, but not both. He swam to the nearer one and deliberately swam past it, until he reached the further one. Tide and current

28

'He swam to the nearer one and deliberately swam past it'

had swept them a long way out and because of a deep creek, now full and spilling over, I could not follow. Beyond the creek was a little sandy bay, not yet covered by the tide. The old dog swam to this bay and put the wigeon down well above the tide line.

The other wigeon (the nearer one) was now opposite him. He wheeled round and swam out to this one, which he brought back and lay beside the first in the sandy bay. At once he picked up the first and swimming the flooded creek brought it to hand. He needed no instructions from me, indeed, throughout, I was but a spectator. He turned swam back over the creek, picked the other duck, now almost awash, and brought that back.

I think that was the best performance that I have ever seen in the shooting field.

One place where I used to do the morning flight was far out on the mud at low tide. I sat this wonderful old dog about 70 yards out at my side to act as a flanker, a job he understood well. If I shot a duck he would remain at his post. If one came down, obviously only wounded, he would leave his post,

29

hunt for and retrieve the duck and then return to his flanking position. That shows considerable intelligence. Like many shooting dogs, he knew a wounded bird from a miss and few wounded duck ever escaped him. In deep water he would plunge his head under and more or less dive for a winged duck that thought it had escaped him.

I paid an annual rent of 25 shillings for the shooting over half a dozen fields. There was no game on these fields, but after a wet spell some flashes formed and usually the dog and I would return with a dozen wigeon.

This great dog came to me when I was working for the Forestry Commission in Thetford forest in East Anglia – my first appointment. One of our foresters had a lovely black labrador bitch that I admired. 'If the old bitch ever has puppies, may I have one, please?' 'Oh yes, she's in pup now.' 'What is the father?' 'One of the blue-blooded labs from The Hall' (The Hall was Lynford Hall, then occupied by Sir James Calder, a great shooting man).

In due course the pups were born. I went to choose mine. Choosing a puppy is always difficult. Some people choose the largest. I look very carefully at the smallest, for such a puppy soon learns that he needs guile to get a feed from the bitch, when his stronger and heavier brothers and sisters are competing. I chose the smallest, really the runt of the litter. He was bright of eye and very alert.

He was one of those wonderful puppies that hardly needs any training. He took his lessons almost for granted and he had an inborn knowledge of the ways of game. He retrieved his first tennis ball, as a tiny puppy, on the day that King George V died.

His first day out with a gun was on a small grouse moor that I managed in Wales. The first grouse of the day got up at my feet and fell dead 30 yards out. The puppy sat as good as gold, for I had trained him to sit whenever I mounted the gun. He had marked that grouse to an inch and, when told, he raced out, picked it cleanly, and returned fast. I do not know how many grouse I shot over him during his lifetime, but it was a very large number, as he became a fine grouse dog.

That same first day I tinkered a grouse that got up on the edge of the moor when I was outside gun. The bird was wing-tipped and went down in the middle of a huge bed of bracken that was below and out of sight, under the edge of the moor.

I sent the young dog. I could see his progress from the movement of the bracken. He went like an arrow into the middle of the bracken bed, and then turned and came straight back. He had not worked the ground at all, but he returned with that grouse.

Such moments stay in one's mind forever and that was one of the happiest shooting days of my life.

Very many years later, I was training his son, Brent, on another moor. A grouse rose and I fluffed it. Away went Brent (well, has *your* dog never run-in?) but the Wog just stood, his eyes glued to the wounded bird. In due course that grouse towered and fell dead some 300 yards or more away. By then, Brent was returning very ashamed of himself. I just whispered to the old dog: 'Get on!' and away he went. He had marked the towered bird exactly and went to it as if it was lying in the middle of a bare tennis court – nothing remarkable about that retrieve: it was just routine for him.

After war broke out, the old Colonel for whom I managed the other moor, telephoned. 'Arthur', he said, 'none of us will get any shooting again for a very long time. Go up to the moor and shoot what you can for the larder.' It was some time before I had any time to spare, and then, one Saturday I managed a couple of hours. I knew the moor well and I remembered where every covey had risen on the Twelfth that year, when eight guns had shot 8 brace. I decided that I would try to find each covey, rather than try to cover the whole moor.

I took both dogs, father and son, and they worked beautifully and I shot well above my normal form. We found covey after covey, and two hours later I was back at the car with 10½ brace. A wonderful outing of splendid dog work and excellent sport. Without my two dogs I would have been lucky to shoot a brace.

Now, over 50 years later, I think I could go back to every place that we found birds on that memorable day!

Sir Wintringham Stable, who later became a famous High Court Judge, was a great dog man. Always he was accompanied by at least eight Welsh springers, all under perfect control. (How many shooting men can keep one spaniel under perfect control?) Old Booby, a very old intelligent labrador accompanied them, but he was allowed to do more or less what he liked. How well I remember him having his own bit of sport on the moor! He worked carefully, and then pounced. There was a squeal as he caught and killed a rat, an unlikely victim on a grouse moor!

It was a year or two before I had a chance to return to East Anglia for a day's shooting. I telephoned the forester and invited him to come round and have a drink and to see his puppy.

'Well!' he exclaimed, as he looked at the dog, 'Fancy him turning out like that! And his father was only the parsons's old terrier!' He had forgotten about the alleged blue-blooded sire from the Hall. But the old dog was no beauty. His ears were sometimes slightly pricked and he had a thin white line on his chest.

I told that story to the Judge, who thought very highly of my dog, and whose praise I valued more than any other man's. 'All I can say,' he replied, 'is that the parson ought to be made a bishop!'

I could fill a whole book with stories about this wonderful dog, whose exploits with geese were numerous too.

When he was a really old dog, the guns were moving between the first and second drives on a well-known moor. The route passed a mountain lake where a duck often lurked in the reed bed and the host always encouraged the leading guns to put in a cartridge so as to be ready for a duck. On this occasion a teal rose and several shots were fired. The teal, hit, fell dead a long way out on the lake. All the dogs present were sent: two yellow labradors, a chocolate labrador, several black labradors including my old dog in his last year, and the Judge's eight spaniels.

There was a gale blowing and nasty waves. One after another the other dogs turned back, leaving my old dog, with his grey muzzle set, heading for the dead teal. He picked it some 150 yards down wind and then, instead of battling his way against the gale, he set off aslant across the wind. That took him a very long way down the shore. He came back slowly, the teal held high, and when he was near, the Judge had his eight spaniels sitting in a semi-circle. As I took the teal from his old muzzle, the Judge turned to his spaniels and said: 'There, the old man's worth the whole lot of you put together. He's the Best Dog in the World!,' and the old dog's brown old eyes shone with pride! Certainly he was the best dog that I have ever known, except Tiro.

Tiro was a German Wachtel belonging to my friend Horst Künne, that great artist sportsman. On my many visits to Horst to 'hunt' wild boar, I established a close rapport with Tiro. He was a truly great dog. Primarily he was a deer dog and local sportsmen who had wounded a deer would telephone Horst, who would take Tiro, *the next day*, to the place where the deer had been lost. It was very rare indeed for Tiro to fail to find the wounded beast, on a cold line that might take two hours to work out. But he was a good all-round dog with a shotgun too. I have to admit that Tiro was the best dog that I have ever known. My old dog was never a deer dog, but on wildfowl and game, I have known no better dog.

I have had one superb deer dog – Mole. It so happened that when Bear, my famous goose dog, was killed on a railway line, there was a litter of young puppies that were his half brothers and sisters. I went to see them even though I had decided not to have another puppy, but when this little black mite came stumbling down the path to me, he looked so like Bear, as a puppy, that I could not resist him. Bear had never been interested in deer, but I decided to make Mole my companion when stalking. He became a fine deer dog and his fame was almost international, as many foreign sportsmen met him and stalked with him. He became quite a good wildfowl dog, too, but he was useless with game when he was almost totally uncontrollable.

Not so with deer. He would stalk with me, his nose against my left knee. When he winded a deer he would nudge me, and I could tell from the way he pointed his nose and wrinkled it, almost precisely where the deer was. Alas he could not tell me whether it was a buck or doe, but we stalked many a deer in thick cover and got within ten or fifteen yards of it – and away again, if it was one we did not wish to shoot.

I remember one morning I was stalking with a Belgian friend. There was a nice old buck that used to feed amongst alders along the bottom of a dingle. Each side was a crop of dense Norway spruce about six to eight feet high. In order to see the buck in one of the glades amongst the alders, we had to stalk up the burn through the spruce.

It was a glorious summer morning, but it had rained heavily the night before and every needle of each spruce tree carried drops of water, glistening like diamonds in the first rays of the sun. We were wet to the skin in a few yards. The little valley was framed on the left side by a grassy bank. We were half way long this bank, keeping under it, when Mole put up his nose and pointed to the left.

I told my chasseur: 'He tells me there's a doe feeding on the ride over the top of the bank. Creep up and have a look. It might be the buck.' Of course I knew that a doe fed there daily. So it proved to be the case, but my friend was very impressed.

We reached the bottom of the alders where I knew the old buck lived, often accompanied by a yearling. Mole stood and pointed to a glade on the left. Then he swung to the right indicating another. I could tell from his wrinkling nose that the right one was further away.

I whispered: 'He tells me there are two bucks ahead, one a yearling, the other an old shootable beast. Go slowly forward to the left one. If it is the yearling, as Mole thinks, come back without disturbing him and we'll stalk the other.' It was the yearling, and my friend returned, very soon. We stalked the other, Mole telling us precisely where he was standing – and, sure enough, there he was broadside on. At the shot, the buck fell, but immediately jumped to his feet and was off. I sent Mole and a little while later we could hear him with the buck, holding him, and that was that.

Of course Mole's reputation was made for ever. My friend thought that he was the most intelligent deer dog in the world. Not only had he told me the sex of the deer we had seen later, but, in my friend's mind, he had distinguished a shootable buck from a young one and also recovered the wounded buck. But Mole had only told me where the three deer had been standing. I already knew their sex and quality.

Often, after a morning's stalk, I have been sitting smoking a cigar to upset the midges, relaxed and happy in the early morning's beauty, when Mole has nudged my knee. And a deer would emerge where he was looking.

'Mole telling us precisely where he was standing'

Once, before the red deer season had opened, we had had a blank morning. I was lying on a heather knoll, when Mole nudged me. Almost at once a fine red stag stepped out of a thicket about 50 yards away and stood surveying the world. Poor dog, he could not understand why I did not raise my rifle!

He loved fishing. If I was casting a dry fly to a rising trout on the right and he saw another good rise on the left, he would nudge me and point to the second fish. I am sure that he could have been trained to retrieve fish, but I would not let him try. A landing net is more efficient.

Bear was a great goose dog. His introduction to wildfowl came when he was only 5½ months old on his first September 1st. (I know that no professional dog trainer would take a dog into the shooting field at such an early age. But I have always thought that experience for a wildfowl dog, if already obedient, is what counts most – and anyway I knew that I would need a dog that morning!) He retrieved his first mallard, wigeon, teal, tufted, snipe, pigeon and also his first partridge on that September morning, so long ago. All except the partridge and the pigeon, were fetched from the waters of the loch, the first ducks dragged back by the wing, although he soon learnt how to carry properly.

His first goose was on Solway. I had gone out very early and found the hole I intended to occupy only 150 yards from a mass of geese. I thought I was the only fowler, as indeed I was at that hour. But, presently a mass of gunners arrived shouting to each other, flashing lights and putting up all the geese. What had seemed a certainty was now hopeless, and I was surrounded by what might have been a football rabble at a big match.

One goose, a single pink, crossed the shoreline appearing from the direction of Criffel, when the flight by normal standards should have been over. It flew straight for me, not too high, but at a pleasing height to achieve. At my shot it fell, dead, on the green merse 50 yards behind, and some 50 envious heads came up out of their hiding places, looking like neeps (turnips). Nothing looks so unnatural on mudflat or salting as a human face!

I sent the now overgrown pup and he went straight to the dead goose and came back with it, tail wagging proudly, as well as any dog could have done. Alas I had no camera, but that memory will last for ever.

Bear developed a great knowledge of geese. He soon knew where a wounded goose was likely to hide, or, more important, where a goose on water that had dived was likely to emerge again. On the open shore many of his retrieves were from a distance of a quarter of a mile or more – and many of his exploits are history.

I will relate one fabulous retrieve. I was standing amongst sallow bushes in a rough marsh, waiting for the evening flight, Bear sitting beside me. A skein of greys came over, high. At my shot, a big gander started to plane down. I could see he would hit the ground 300 or 400 yards away and knowing well all this vast area of scrub and marsh, I thought that I knew exactly whereabouts he would be. I sent Bear, and off he went full of confidence. Then I decided to go too, to show him where to work.

I had not gone far before I heard him returning. He passed me, carrying the goose (a very good retrieve) without seeing me, and headed for the place where I had been. Obviously he put down the goose there, and followed my scent, and he re-joined me very quickly, without the goose. We returned to my shooting stick and bag. Bear stared at the ground with an expression of amazement on his face. The goose was no longer there!

It was a foolish goose that thought he could outwit Bear, even in 400 acres or so of dense cover. Off the dog went, again, on the line of the goose and it was not long before he had it back safely and securely. This was typical of Bear's retrieves. He seemed to know just where a goose would come down and he needed no human help to find it.

When his life ended in front of a train, everyone who knew him was devastated. He was a lovely dog and great companion, and a fine wildfowl dog with a speciality for geese. His end came through my own fault. I had taken out a young lad for his first wigeon flight on saltings near a minor railway line. I left Simon with Bear. 'Keep him on the lead. He will find anything you shoot', I said.

The first bird fell over the railway line and Simon took Bear, on the lead, over the line and then released the dog to look for it. I myself was 100 yards or so away, further up the line, training Honey who was a young dog then. Bear found the bird and brought it to Simon. Then, as I should have foreseen, he ran along the line, looking for me. Just then one of the few trains came.

There was not a mark on him and I hoped against hope that he was only stunned. But he was dead. I carried him back with anguish in my heart. I buried him by the pond, in the arboretum, together with the last bird of his retrieving career. Every spring, mallard breed on this pond and the ducklings swim to and fro beside his grave. There, too lie Honey and Mole.

Honey became a great all-round shooting man's dog and a very good goose dog too. She had many excellent retrieves in her career, and she would wear down the lightest wounded goose by sheer persistence, however far from land it had swum. The longest swim never seemed to tire her, even although she was only a small labrador, far less strong than Bear had been.

We used to shoot the island on the final day of the season, only. On my last occasion there, I was with Honey who had never flighted the island before. In the very last light a final grey came past and, only wing tipped, it glided down onto the loch a long way off. Honey went at once. I did not know whether she would get that goose as the area of the loch was vast. But my worry was where would she end up? If she reached the shore with that goose, would she go looking for me along the shore?

I waited and waited, my anxiety increasing with every moment. Then there was a ripple and her old face shoved the goose to my feet.

It is the case that most shooting dogs know by instinct where their master is standing when they are sent for a retrieve. Mole, after seeking a wounded deer, would always return to the spot from which he had started. That was what Honey had done with that greylag, and I need not have worried.

Dogs have more intelligence than many humans think they have. But it is a mistake to credit them with a human's reasoning powers. How often one hears 'The damn dog knows exactly what he has done wrong' – thwack thwack and yowl yowl – when the dog has not got a clue as to why he is being beaten.

IV

SCENT

ALAS, man has lost the ability to scent his quarry in the way that 'hunted' animals, such as deer, can scent him. Deer have most efficient powers of scenting their enemy and that is one reason why hill walkers in red deer country do so much harm. It is not their vivid red, green or blue anoraks which do the damage, for deer are colour blind, but their 'scent' will clear all deer downwind of them for a very great distance. In times of harsh weather and food shortage, it is serious for the deer to be moved from the most sheltered and best feeding areas. Also, hinds have certain calving zones, no doubt chosen because the conditions are best suited for the new born calves. If such areas are frequently made sterile of deer, because hill walkers give their wind to them, then the health of the herd is likely to suffer over future years through weaker calves being reared. Spoiling a stalk by moving deer which are about to be culled, because they have winded hill walkers, is also harmful. Too many deer numbers in many areas in the Highlands can only be put right by a heavier cull of the hinds.

The scenting dogs are of the highest quality. My old stalking dog, Mole would tell whether a deer was 200 yards away, eighty yards – or twenty, by the way he wrinkled his nose, but first he would nudge my knee to draw my attention.

It is difficult for a man to begin to understand the vagaries of scent. But constant observation of his dogs, when working, will give certain indications. Different dogs (and indeed different animals) have different scenting qualities. I have an idea that a dog with long bristles on his muzzle has better scenting powers than a dog with scanty bristles. Perhaps a man with a long untidy moustache can scent his bacon at breakfast time more readily than his clean-shaven brother. It must be appreciated that different dogs have different expertise in using their noses, and that experience over the years makes some dogs more proficient than others.

Jorrocks was right when he said: 'There's nothing so queer as scent, 'cept

'. . . .a dog with long bristles on his muzzle has better scenting powers'

a woman'! There are certain facts which concern scent and H.M. Budgett, after long and careful research wrote a book, *Hunting by Scent* (1933, Eyre and Spottiswood), which uncovers most of its mysteries.

The majority of animals either sweat through, or have glands in, their feet. But game birds do not have such glands and it is likely that when squatting, scent glands in their body impregnate their feet with body scent.

Any bird or animal, including man, leaves a trail of scent particles on the ground, or on herbage where the feet have trodden or which has been touched by the body in passing. Scent is the air which has come into contact with these particles, not the particles themselves.

The best scenting conditions are when air currents carry the scent towards the dog: where the air is rising and moving downwind. Climatic conditions, which vary with each day, and locality, affect scenting, although there appears to be no direct connection between scent and barometric pressure. Hot air rises, therefore when the temperature at the ground (i.e., immediately below the surface) is higher than that of the air above it, scenting conditions are good. When the temperature at the ground is lower than that of the air above, there will be little or no scent. The earth seems to absorb air under these conditions. If the temperature of the air and the earth are equal, then scenting conditions will be average.

What are the factors which influence the above-mentioned scenting conditions? Mist or fog occur when moist ground conditions are at a higher temperature than the air, and water tends to retard loss of heat. Therefore scenting conditions may be expected to be good in mist.

After a mild spell, a frost cools the air whilst the ground radiates some warmth and this should give good scenting conditions. This aids predators to find their prey, which feed at dusk, but it also helps the potential prey to scent its predators. That is why deer prefer to feed upwind, when they can scent danger ahead.

A change from a warm westerly wind to a cold east wind also produces good scenting conditions. If snow falls before a frost the ground remains warm and scent should be good; if snow falls on frozen ground scent will be bad until well after the thaw. After prolonged frost and hard weather, the thaw will be accompanied by warm air and, often, gale force winds, which are good for wildfowling, but not for scent.

White hoar frost on the cobwebs means that the ground temperature will be lower than air temperature, with poor scenting conditions.

On the same day with the same weather, one may encounter different scenting conditions in different places. In the open, the ground may be warmed by the sun, whilst the air is still cooler, and scent will be good. But in woodland, shade will keep the ground cool and scent will be poor. The reverse happens when a warm breeze heats the air in the open, but not in the shade in covert. But if the soil retains heat from the previous day, scent will be all right.

To put these generalities more precisely, when the air temperature is two or three degrees warmer than that of the soil, there should be a moderate scent. If the air is five or six degrees warmer, scent will be very poor and at ten degrees warmer it will be non-existent.

During the day, conditions change all the time. The earth is not subject to rapid change, three or four degrees during the day only. But air temperature may change as much as twenty degrees.

Heavy rain may wash out or obliterate scent; intense cold may retard it; bright sunlight may obscure scent for several hours; bright daylight may deodorise scent, so the best conditions for photography may be the worst for scenting.

It follows from these facts, which often mean poor scenting conditions between noon and 3 pm, that at field trials dogs working early and late in the day may have an advantage over those working in the middle of the day.

There are other factors which affect scenting conditions. A newly carted hay field, fields with cattle fed on cowcake, rushes and green bracken often hold but little scent. Willowherb, garlic and wild mint, in flower, are bad conditions for scent as is a crop of mustard, or burnt stubble.

When a man or deer walks across a dew-soaked lawn, a marked track is left for all to see. This is known as foil. When there is no dew this track will still be there, but it requires a very expert eye to see it, as the only evidence is the grass that is pressed flat. However crushed grass or other vegetation gives off its own scent and a dog is able to follow this line, sometimes better than the animal's own scent.

Wounded animals give off a scent from particles of blood. This is the scent that one wants one's dog to distinguish from the fresh scent of unwounded animals. A wounded animal, especially a stag during the rut, calls upon reserves of adrenalin from which it draws extra strength. It may be assumed that a dog, hunting the wounded animal, is aware of this too.

The scent derived from different animals lasts for different periods. A fox's scent lasts for half an hour on average, a hare's for 45 minutes, a bird's for two hours and a man's for five hours, a deer's for six hours and a wild boar's for twelve hours. The scent particles from an otter are very fatty and his scent may last for two days. Blood scent from a wounded animal lasts longest. But of course local conditions will cause the above average times to vary. The subject is one of very great interest.

Because of man's very inferior scenting powers, every sportsman who works dogs should never forget that his lack of scenting powers puts him at a great disadvantage, when his dog needs help and encouragement. How often does one see a man with a gun and several beaters milling round where a bird is believed to have fallen, thus spoiling the scent and making the dog's task more difficult!

Often when the dog is working the line of a runner, man, in his ignorance, believes the bird to have gone in a different direction. If your dog is experienced, leave it to him. He knows what he is doing. However, a dog should be directed to work into the wind when this is possible: all humans should keep out of his way.

Both bird dogs and retrieving dogs need to become masters of the art of scenting. They must be fearless in cover and those that retrieve must be good swimmers. These dogs will soon learn that water carries the scent down stream.

Bird dogs should learn to adjust their behaviour to the scenting conditions. When scent is good, a pointer will range more widely than when bad. On bad scenting days he must work up wind and cover the ground very closely, or game will be missed.

A man working pointers and setters may be faced with a difficult choice: shall he work his dogs towards the march fence (boundary) because poor scent dictates that as best, or should he risk not flushing them at all?

Where retrieves are concerned, on bad scenting days, the sooner the dog can be sent, the better his chances. Of course marking a wounded bird accurately is most important. Some dogs excel at this: some men are hopeless!

If a dead bird lies tail to wind, then the ruffled feathers will allow the wind to carry more scent than there is from a dead bird lying head to wind, with its feathers tightly in place.

Besides the intricacies of scent there is one other common occurrence which is very difficult to explain – that is dowsing, or water divining. Many things other than the discovery of water may be done with a hazel rod. Dowsers, by carrying an article of clothing of the missing person, have been able to locate bodies. I have followed a wounded deer by holding blood stained soil in my hand. But it is not easy to follow a line.

To sum up: scent is a very complex subject. Have faith in your dog and do not make his job more difficulty by thoughtless human activity!

'If your dog is experienced, leave it to him'

V

DOGS AND LAUGHTER

NEARLY all dogs smile, but that is more an expression of pleasure, rather than amusement. That great sportsman Jim Corbett relates how, when he unexpectedly arrived within eight feet of a man-eating tigress, on her face was a smile, similar to that of a dog welcoming his master home. (She was not laughing because her dinner had arrived by accident almost between her paws!) Dogs sometimes appear to be laughing with their human companions. Usually this is because, inadvertently, they have done something to make those around them laugh, and every dog likes to be the centre of attention. But a dog never likes being ridiculed and laughed at unkindly.

It is my experience that a large dog is more likely to do things which cause amusement. They tend to have something of a buffoon in their make up, and this was particularly true of dear old Nigger, an enormous black labrador. How well I remember the first day's pheasant shooting after World War II at which I was a guest. Nigger had not attended such a day before. My host had acquired a new car (as rare as the crown jewels in those difficult days). At one stage he asked me to drive this car to the next stand. No way was I going to put a large muddy labrador into a brand new car, so I got a friend to take Nigger in a Land Rover. By the time we met up again, the guns were already lined up at their pegs at the edge of a field of turnips ('neeps', in Scotland). Nigger was so delighted to see me again, that he ran up and down the line of guns seizing the odd neep and throwing it high in the air, or else bringing it to me as a welcoming present. Everyone roared with laughter!

Drex, another huge dog, a yellow labrador, was so often a source of much amusement. His name originated from the fact that when he was a puppy he was exactly like the Andrex puppy. Although so big, his huge lovable head seemed to be full of sawdust rather than brains. He became a good goose dog and he would carry a greylag as lesser dogs would carry a teal.

'Nigger was so delighted to see me again'

One day I took a keeper friend out on the mud after geese. When the flight was over he told me that he had a goose down far out on the mud. He had no dog with him and not wanting the long muddy walk myself, I said: 'Take Drex', who was attached to my goose bag by the lead. So saying, I took off the bag and passed it to my friend, who put it over his shoulder and walked off. Drex never so much as glanced at me, and I was somewhat surprised, and hurt, that he had transferred his allegiance so casually.

I watched them trailing off across the mud. After about a hundred yards they came to a sudden halt. As they were nowhere near where the goose was, I put my field glasses up. Drex had suddenly realised that he was no longer attached to me. He refused, point blank to go another yard with someone he did not know. That goose was never picked!

Drex's training was never what it should have been. Two other very good shooting dogs made it unnecessary to train a third. I decided to introduce him to deer. Some young red deer had been knocking hell out of

44

a field of barley, so I went out one evening to try to sort them out. I took Drex and we crept into a small hollow in the corner of the next field, about fifty yards from the rough woodland from which the deer were wont to come. On our left and a little forward was a large oak tree and the wind blew from the tree, behind which was the path of the deer, to Drex and myself.

Drex curled up and went to sleep. Presently a roe doe came out. I had no wish to shoot her, but I was interested to see how Drex would react when she reached a point where her wind would be blown to us, as every shooting outing which Drex ever had, had been at pigeons, duck or geese, all quarry which he had learnt flew high and wide.

When the doe was behind the oak tree, his nose began to wrinkle. 'That's a nice smell!' was his obvious reaction. He sat up and stared into the crown of the oak tree, thinking that this new quarry must be high in the air and he was obviously puzzled when he could see nothing of interest. The red deer did not come out, so he did not see a deer shot.

The first time he accompanied me fishing, he took little or no interest in the proceedings. I got into a 2 lb rainbow and this nice fish was just coming to the net, when Drex became aware of the proceedings. He took a flying leap from the top of the bank and landed, all four feet, on top of the very surprised fish. I got him out of the loch and by a miracle the rainbow was still 'on' and was duly landed, without further mishap!

At Christmas we used to dress him up as 'Father Drexmas' and he distributed presents from the Christmas tree. He revelled in this task and he did it very well indeed, and was greatly loved by all who knew him.

Cherry, a lively and lovable Jack Russell, came to us from a town, where she saw and walked on only concrete and tarmac, and was fed on cream buns. She took to a country life like a duck to water and became a great ratter. Her three greatest joys in life were Mar's Bars, hunting a mouse in the field, which she pursued with the enthusiasm of a wildfowler for geese, – and chasing cats! She would run after any cat with perseverance: until it stopped. Then she would remember an urgent engagement elsewhere, and disappear. Or if she was lucky enough to 'tree' it she would sit and watch and wait, sometimes for hours! As a result she never received a scratch on her nose or face.

Butty, my present young Happy's grandmother, spent most of her life as a brood bitch, and her young are scattered far and wide, each with attributes which their present owners relate with bated breath. But she was a good game dog. I remember her first retrieve. I had taken her to the edge of the shore, hoping to get a shot at duck, but only a wood pigeon came near. The pigeon fell dead into some thorn bushes. I sent Butty, but she came back with nothing. So I sent her again and watched her try to climb into a thorn bush. The pigeon was stuck up it and by putting her fore-paws on the bole of the tree, she managed to reach it. That was a good retrieve for her first.

Hares were her undoing, especially as she resented the fact that I do not like shooting hares. At a partridge drive, a hare came towards us. It sat up and made faces at us, and Butty took exception to this misguided behaviour. I was outside gun and when the hare bolted past, lickity split, I bowled it over. But it got to its feet again and staggered off, slowly. That was too much for Butty. She was attached to my shooting stick and away she rushed, the stick whirling around her backside. Despite this handicap she caught up with the hare and brought it (and my shooting stick) back to hand, much to the amusement of the other guns.

In later life she became a good picking-up dog. She was a great wildfowl dog and on the river Severn, where we flighted Canada's, she would bring back a wounded gander well, even though she was a small dog.

Sometimes dogs do appear to have a sense of humour – like the famous Field Trial Champion who, when sent in, when all the first class dogs had failed, turned up with a hedgehog in his mouth!

'Sometimes dogs do appear to have a sense of humour'

46

VI

HINTS ON TRAINING
AND CARE

FIRST, one has to decide the breed which will suit the type of shooting one usually enjoys. I am a dedicated labrador man and, for the average wildfowler or duck shooter, a labrador must be high on the list.

It is most important that one's puppy must come from a good working or Field Trial strain. It is generally agreed that performance in the field is passed on by the dam, whereas conformation and looks are passed on by the sire. If possible, one should try to see the bitch concerned actually working. It is useful to see the dog, too, although good looks are not so important for a shooting dog. If there is any history of hip displacement, or blindness, avoid all the puppies.

How to choose a puppy from a litter is something of a problem. The author of *Nature Notes of a Highland Gamekeeper* and *Wildlife of the Highlands*, Dugald MacIntyre, recommends choosing the first born. But at eight weeks old, the first born has merged into a mass of wagging tails and happy puppies, mostly looking alike. So which is the one to choose?

I myself tend to pick the smallest, as that puppy will have learnt how to fend for himself amongst his stronger brothers and sisters, when seeking a meal from the mother. Provided the smallest is healthy and fit, he will make a good choice. The largest puppy may grow too big and tend to be lazy.

A puppy which runs up to one, and shows interest and no fear, is usually a good choice, and the expression in the eyes and face of a puppy is something to go by. If he is nervous of sudden movement or noise (such as clapping hands), he should be avoided. In the case of labradors, the eyes should be the colour of burnt sugar. Any pale, yellow-eyed dog may turn out to have an untrustworthy character.

The question as to whether to choose a dog puppy, or a bitch, is one of personal choice. Many claim that bitches are more biddable and easier to

'. . . the expression in the eyes and face of a puppy is something to go by'

train. But their two periods per year of being in season, for three weeks on each occasion, is a nuisance. One cannot take a bitch in heat to a shoot where other dogs are present, although the frequent application of anti-mate is a deterrent to male dogs that prefer sex to sport! Male puppies may be more obstinate than bitches, and if a male develops aggressiveness towards other dogs, that is an unmitigated nuisance, which will make him very unpopular.

The puppy should be taken between seven and nine weeks old, the natural age for weaning from the dam. At first, in strange surroundings, the puppy will be rather lost and unhappy. He must be made as comfortable and warm as possible and his new master should see to all his needs, especially food. So far as is possible his food should be the same as he is used to having. (Sudden changes in the normal food of any dog may lead to tummy upsets.) The puppy will soon form an attachment to his new master, who, in the canine world, takes the place of the 'leader of the pack' in the wild.

As soon as he has settled down in his new home, some discipline should be imposed. The puppy may be taught to sit before each meal, by pushing him down and giving the firm command 'sit' at the same time. 'Get it' will tell him he may go to his bowl to eat. The same bowl should be used, always, for each dog in the home. The most important word of command for a puppy to learn is 'No'. This command must be obeyed automatically for ever more. But it is essential, as with every command, that the puppy must understand what he is instructed not to do.

Here it is necessary to emphasise that this is the most important consideration in everything that the dog trainer tries to teach. A dog relates words of command, or words of displeasure, to one action. If a dog will not return when called, it is no use chastising him when he does return. He will think that the act of returning is the cause of his master's displeasure. One must try to think with his limited mind. One often hears it said: 'Oh he knows perfectly well what he has done wrong!' So often the poor dog does not know: and that is his master's fault for not understanding the dog's activities.

Hence both bribery and chastisement must be considered carefully by a dog trainer. Bribery by the gift of a tit-bit should only be employed infrequently and chastisement even less frequently. Verbal encouragement and a friendly pat is better than the over use of a biscuit as a reward. Verbal displeasure is more important than physical chastisement. Every puppy soon learns from the tone of voice whether he has pleased, or displeased his master.

So every dog trainer must observe every action of his dog pupil, always with common sense and understanding of a dog's mind and thought processes. Most dogs have an inborn desire to please, and if that desire is frustrated by misunderstandings, a confused, frustrated and, worst of all, nervous puppy may become even more difficult to steer in the direction in which one wishes to develop his natural instincts.

So it is important to observe one's dog at all times and then to ask oneself: why? Why has he done this, or that – or not done something else? At the same time it is fair to say that a dog observes his master, constantly. When rewards are put into his master's pocket, the dog knows exactly in which pocket they are. When teaching a dog to come to the whistle and to earn a reward, that dog will soon notice that his master puts the whistle to his lips and may start to come before the whistle is blown!

It is necessary that a puppy should learn his name, and answer to it. But very soon his name must be replaced, when calling him, by the whistle. The man who shouts his dog's name loudly and frequently in the shooting field will do much to conserve the head of game, and to reduce the bag, and the day's sport! A silent whistle is an advantage, because onlookers do not hear it and therefore they may not notice the dog's disobedience. When the dog is close, a hiss to attract his attention is all that is needed.

49

The question of keeping a puppy in the house or in a kennel is a matter of personal choice. I prefer my dogs to live with me and to accompany me everywhere, at home or in the office. But I suppose that the three most destructive creatures of all are a bull in a china shop, a young child in a choice garden, and a puppy in a house. Like children, puppies all have their different characters and personalities: they also need a great deal of playtime. In a house, no shoes are *ever* safe and it is the most expensive or favourite shoes which become victims of a puppy's sharp teeth. By chance, as I write this, I have received a letter from a companion who helped me to rear and train many puppies, and who, alas, has been dog-less for some time, until she obtained another puppy. I quote: 'You said you were glad I had another puppy. You wouldn't be if you knew the trouble he is! I had forgotten the amount of mischief they can think up and Roo is no exception to that rule!' Perhaps, appropriately, after the two preceding chapters to this one had just been typed, Roo demolished all that completed typing and set back the publication of this book by several days!

The main difficulty in a house is that when a pup runs off with a shoe, a tea towel or perhaps stockings, the owner of such items is liable to give chase in no uncertain manner. It is the instinct of retrieving dogs to pick up and to carry, and, if chased, and admonished, then this retrieving instinct may be impaired or even destroyed and the puppy's future spoilt. Children who play tug o' war with a puppy, or who throw stones or hard objects for the puppy to retrieve may make him hard mouthed.

Puppies may cause an immense amount of damage, even apart from chewing slippers and other things. Long ago when Honey was shut up in the kitchen, she chewed a big hole in the kitchen door, to the delight of the other dogs who used it, until the door was replaced several years later!

Much damage may be done to the upholstery of a car. A puppy should be accustomed to travelling in a car and it should be trained not to get off the floor – or to stay in the back behind a dog guard. Many dog owners have a special box made for their dogs to be kept inside their car or Land Rover.

A dog who worships his master will soon take over his master's chair if not stopped. Each dog should have his own corner.

It is very desirable to train all the dogs in a house not to quarrel over a bone or food bowl. My dogs always share with each other and with other pets. Butty would share a bottle with a bottle-fed lamb!

A puppy kept in a kennel and only exercised by his master will not be subject to these difficulties. The person who exercises a puppy establishes a rapport even more quickly than he who feeds the pup. Puppies by instinct are naturally clean. When accidents happen it is often the master's fault because the pup has not been let out often enough. A puppy needs plenty of exercise and time to play, but he should not become over tired.

When he picks up and carries different things, he should be encouraged to bring them. Indeed soon he may be trained to retrieve a dummy, such as an old glove rolled and tied into a compact object, or a stocking tied up in a similar way, or a ball, (tennis ball size). The dummy must be soft and when the puppy is allowed to make his first retrieve, his master should position himself between the pup and the house or kennel, as it is his natural instinct to take it back home. The dummy must be taken very gently, with the hand below the dummy, and never tugged. If the pup will not release it, gentle pressure on a paw will make him do so.

Such lessons must not be overdone, or the puppy will become bored and lose interest. It is important that obedience to the whistle has already been properly taught. Then, if the puppy runs off with the dummy, or plays with it, he must be whistled to bring it to hand.

Later the dummy may be hidden in a bush or a clump of grass, etc., so that the puppy learns to hunt. Of course a rolling ball leaves a line to follow, or a friend can drag the dummy, thus leaving a line to encourage the use of the puppy's nose. When first starting retrieving lessons, the dummy will be thrown upwind. Later the pupil will learn to cast himself downwind of the dummy.

These then are the elementary beginnings of dog training. Sometimes amateurs do not proceed further and think that the puppy is ready for real work with a gun. That is a mistake and professional dog trainers do not usually get a dog to be trained until he is six months old, or older.

The three faults which are most difficult to correct are gun shyness, running in and, later, whining. A dog which becomes gun shy will react to any sudden noise and cringe away, frightened. A really bad case is usually incurable. If noise shyness has not developed badly, great patience is needed to accustom the puppy to sudden noise. The object is to try to build up confidence, so that the puppy associates noise with something pleasant. The way to achieve this is to make an acceptable sound as a sign that it is feeding time. If the puppy can become accustomed to associate sudden noise with his bowl of food, then this may be done by firing an air rifle in the air. If he gets used to this, a .22 may be substituted and later, perhaps a .410 fired a little distance away. But a really gun shy dog may connect the sight of a weapon with the sound that frightens him. He will then cringe at the sight of a gun. There is but little hope of a cure if this sad stage is reached.

Later, of course, a dog that is not gun shy will learn to connect the discharge of a gun with a bird that is shot – and that is the start of running-in. With a dog that is not gun shy I teach the dog first to 'drop' flat on his stomach at the command to 'drop', or 'down'. The next stage is to mount a stick as if it was a gun, and make the dog drop to the sight of a stick being mounted. Later, when an empty gun is being carried, he will drop automatically when the gun is mounted, and, later still, when the gun is mounted and a dummy thrown at the same time. After that the gun may be fired as the dummy is thrown. At this stage it is best to use a gun that makes less sound than a 12 bore, (.22, .410 etc.,) and it is important that the dog remains down whilst his master collects the dummy. He must not connect the firing of the gun with retrieving a dummy, or later, a shot bird.

If a dog does run in, a check cord will bring him to a sudden, surprised halt. But a dog soon learns when a check cord is attached and when it is not. As I have said, observing his reactions and knowing his personality are important. A dog trainer must always be thinking of means to deal with all incidents that occur.

A puppy will soon learn to wear a collar without noticing it. Every dog must be taught to walk on a lead *without pulling*. That is important and should be an early lesson in a puppy's career.

The next stage is teaching a dog to walk to heel when not on the lead. Many amateurs find this difficult and I would assess this as one of the most necessary lessons of all. The dog should be kept on a short lead (especially if the dog pulls to one side) as one walks fairly fast, and commanded to 'heel' with a sharp jerk on the lead. When at heel the dog's nose should be close to his master's left knee and the lead should be held in the left hand. (Or the reverse, in the case of the gun being left-handed.) Much patience and firmness and repetition may be needed. When the dog understands what is wanted and is walking to heel, the lead may be gently dropped. Eventually he should walk to heel on all occasions when required to do so. It is one thing to walk to heel on the training ground with no distractions, and another in the shooting field when game is being flushed and shot all around him. This is a most important part of any dog's training. In traffic, or in a town, a dog which breaks heel, because it has seen something of interest across the road (e.g., another dog) may cause a nasty accident and even lose his life!

'Every dog must be taught to walk on a lead without pulling'

A whining dog is extremely difficult to cure; I have tried nearly everything. But if a dog has been taught the word 'No', then a firm 'NO' at the moment when he starts to whine may be successful. A tap on the nose will emphasise the command. A whining dog is most irritating, not only to the master, but to all in earshot and a dog with this fault cannot be used for deer stalking.

Dogs must be taught to sit and stay. He will have been taught to sit already. He should be made to sit by some mark on the ground – a stump, stone, rock, bush etc. The command 'stay' should be given with the trainer in front of, and facing the dog, with the right hand raised. Retreat one or two paces. If the dog moves from the original position he must be taken back to the exact place near the mark on the ground, and made to sit again, with the command 'stay' repeated. Return slowly to the dog and make him sit and stay again, if he moves. Gradually retreat to a greater distance, until he becomes reliable at staying when told. Later he may be whistled up and, indeed, this is one way of improving his keenness to answer the whistle. An occasional reward may be allowed, but always verbal encouragement, and perhaps a pat, is better than the bribery of a reward. He should come right up to you before being praised.

Regarding the whistle, there are two main things for him to learn to obey: *stop* – a long drawn out whistle, and *come here* – a series of short, sharp blasts. The sit, stay and come here lessons should be repeated several times a day, until he is reliable at this lesson.

Although puppies need a considerable play time and all dogs need to run free for a little while, if only to empty themselves, a dog should not be allowed to run free over the countryside or his obedience will suffer. He may be allowed and even encouraged to hunt in thick cover especially for a dummy, but he must not be allowed to roam everywhere. If he tends to run wild he must be called in and made to walk to heel again.

All this is basic training of great importance. It cannot be stressed too much that all words of command should be given clearly and firmly, and the same words for each command must *always* be used, by everyone who takes out the dog.

In training one's own dog there are so many pleasures and, often, disappointments. The disappointments are usually, at least partly, the fault of the trainer.

In training a dog beyond this point it is best to turn to an expert professional trainer for advice. Such advice will be found in those books mentioned in the chapter 'Dogs in Literature'.

So far as the care of one's dog is concerned, it is important that a dog should be warm and comfortable. That does not mean that a dog needs to be cossetted. A dry wooden bench in a draught-free place is sufficient. Straw is not necessary and it harbours pests. Newspaper makes adequate bedding, if required and it should be changed frequently. Working dogs must be dried at the end of the day and newspaper is also the best means of doing this. When travelling home, the dog should be comfortable and warm. A tired dog should have a short rest before being fed and clean water should always be available. There are many good balanced dog meals to use as a basic food, to which some of the meat in the various reputable tinned dog meats should be added. One can obtain dried meat for dog food, too.

Each dog should be fed at the same time each day and he should have his own dog bowl. No other dog should be allowed to interfere with him, when eating. Over feeding must be avoided.

All puppies must have the various injections which the vet will recommend and give him. Dog fleas can be a nuisance, but there are efficient preventions and cures. A soapy bath is a good idea given during warm weather. Worming is necessary from time to time and drops in the ear will prevent ear trouble. A dog that shakes his head a lot may have ear canker. Cuts, bites and broken skin must be attended to at once and, if very bad, treated by a vet. If a dog has the misfortune to have distemper, the vet must treat the dog. The dog should be considered as seriously ill and a long rest is necessary.

Dogs moult twice a year and at these times, especially, frequent brushing is necessary. A small battery-powered brush which sucks in the loose hairs is on the market, and dogs soon learn to like being brushed by this.

As with all things connected with keeping a dog, common sense is important at all times.

VII

THE DEER DOG

IN most forms of shooting in Britain the recovery of lost game by well-trained dogs is well organised and efficient. Indeed dog work is an important part of a day's shooting. This is not so in the case of woodland stalking, where far too few roe stalkers use a deer dog.

In medieval times roe were not classed as Beasts of the Chase and it is only in recent times that roe have been accorded the position that they have held on the Continent for so long – as a great sporting quarry to be shot only by rifle. In Germany the use of an efficient deer dog is usual, and field trials for deer dogs are held.

Anyone who stalks woodland deer without a dog is foolish, for three reasons. First he risks the horror of losing a wounded deer (anyone who says he has never failed to place the bullet correctly is either an inexperienced stalker, or a still less experienced liar! Probably he will wound one the next time he goes out). If he has placed the bullet in the heart he may still lose the dead deer in dense cover: or it may have dropped in a ploughed forest furrow.

Secondly he will not experience the great excitement of stalking an unseen deer which the dog has told him about. Third, he will miss that wonderful rapport (more so than in any other form of dog work) which develops between a deer dog and his master, when they stalk together frequently.

What breed of dog is most suitable? If the stalker only goes after deer infrequently, then he will not have enough work for a full-time deer dog. He will have to compromise and use his game dog, training him as best he can to adjust to deer. But there will be some degree of conflict between the dog's training for game and his need to concentrate one hundred per cent on deer when stalking. Maybe it will suffice to leave the dog in the car as an insurance against a lost deer. But such a compromise is unsatisfactory, especially for the dog!

Let us assume that the stalker has enough stalking to justify training a full-time deer dog. The breed of dog he chooses will be governed to some extent by the species of deer that he expects to encounter. If he is likely to stalk fallow or sika, or woodland red deer, then he must select one of the larger breeds: labrador, Alsatian, sheepdog, German pointer or Munsterlander – a very fine German sporting dog – or many of the other German breeds.

But if his activities are confined to roe, then smaller breeds are suitable. If most shooting will be done from high seats, then a dog of a small breed, which can be carried on to the seat in a bag, or in a simple harness, is an advantage. A large dog can be trained to sit at the foot of the seat, and that is not difficult. But there is a serious risk that he will be winded by the very buck you would have shot had he not been there.

Suitable small breeds are terriers and daschunds ('teckels'). The small breeds are easier to follow, because they run more slowly than the large breeds and they are unlikely to run mute when following a blood scent. However it is more difficult for them to hold a wounded deer.

A beagle makes a splendid deer dog and spaniels can be good too, although they are tempted to hunt other game.

I have never owned a vizsla but I am sure that it could be trained as an efficient deer dog. Their colour is so like that of the summer coat of a roe, that, when one is barking at a buck to hold him, if he had a glimpse of the dog that might bring him fast!

Labradors tend to run mute. That can be overcome by the use of a bell

'Small breeds are easier to follow'

57

attached to the collar. A beagle may become mute when he comes up to a dead deer. It is most desirable that a deer dog should bark loudly at the culmination of his 'hunt'. The best way to induce a mute dog to bark is to let him be present when another dog is barking at a dead deer. At first he may be a little frightened, and one can tease him by jerking the dead deer's head towards him and tempting him to seize it by the neck. One can also bark at the deer oneself, which will surprise the dog, if it does nothing else. But a deer dog must be silent when one is stalking a deer and, of course, any whining must be stopped at once.

The training of every deer dog must start with standard basic discipline. Most dog trainers do not start serious training until the puppy is a year old. I believe in starting at the beginning. Puppies should be taught to sit at meal times as soon as they are old enough to feed out of a bowl. With deer dogs, ultimately all commands must be by signal. It is no use shouting 'come here you great big something brute and sit down,' when you are about to take the shot. Come to that it is no use making a great speech to any dog at any time. 'Sit' is enough and, later, the dog must learn to sit at a hand signal or at a low hiss. The dog must be taught to walk to heel, but a deer dog should walk to heel with his hind quarters level with one's left knee. Then one can watch his face and his expression all the time. When stalking there will be a 'thread' of mental understanding between dog and man. The dog must be trained to stop, standing, whenever the stalker stops and to move forward again, slowly and steadily, matching his master's speed. He should sit when the stalker starts to take his shot, as he begins to mount the rifle. He must not move then, nor indeed when field glasses are being used. There will be times when the dog must 'stay' for some time. All these are elementary, but essential points of training, and the dog must be thoroughly obedient.

It is very important that the young deer dog should be taught to follow a blood line only, and not to run the line of an unwounded deer. I believe in starting this lesson at an early stage, even before the other lessons have been completely learnt. It is very simple, provided one has first shot a roe (with the dog not present). Tie a soft cloth, or even sphagnum moss, soaked in blood, at the bottom of a thumb stick. Then walk forward putting the stick to the ground as comes naturally when walking. This will simulate the drops of blood falling from a running deer at about one yard apart. Some say that it is necessary to separate the blood scent from that of oneself by dragging a bloody article suspended from a cord held by two people twenty feet apart. This is not necessary. The dog will very soon prefer to follow the blood scent to all other scents, especially if rewarded at the end by a small piece of liver. But the dog must not come to expect a reward each time. After the first time if the dog has succeeded, then future trails should be laid downwind.

It is important that a young dog should progress from a laid blood trail to a real one as soon as possible. This is because the blood scent from a wounded, or heart shot deer will be mixed with the natural scent from the scent glands in the feet. When the blood scent has become very faint, an experienced deer dog will be following that individual deer's scent glands, which have a longer lasting scent than blood. The sooner a young dog becomes aware of this extra, important scent, the better, but *only* when it is mixed with the blood scent.

In Germany the deer dog is fitted with a harness and a leather lead up to twenty feet long. This is an advantage for the handler, attached to the other end. But the dog has to be checked frequently in order for the handler to keep up and on a stale scent this will interfere with the dog's concentration. When following a blood trail he needs to concentrate on that, and nothing else. Also, in a dense stand of sitka spruce, dog and handler will soon become snarled up.

Following a blood line is the pre-eminent lesson because recovering a wounded deer is the most important job that a deer dog has to do. Once the dog has learnt what is required, then a delay of two hours or more between laying the trail and setting him on it should become normal.

When training to stalk, every time the dog shows an interest in following a fresh deer, hare, rabbit or pheasant, he must be checked with a firm 'No'. Indeed that is the only verbal word of command that should be used. It may be necessary to take a young dog into a rabbit pen, or amongst hand-reared pheasants, to check him from taking an interest in either.

He must be introduced to a shot as any dog should be – first an air rifle, then a .22, and a .410 and so on. If he shows signs of fear (which is unusual) this can be overcome by firing the air rifle, or .22, at the time of feeding.

Later he should sit beside one when one is shooting at a target. It is absolutely essential at all times to ensure that the muzzle of the rifle is nowhere near a dog's head. If the dog is too near the rifle, when one is about to shoot *the* buck, let the buck go, rather than risk the dog's ear drums.

A dog that has been trained for deer, should not be used for game until he is at least two years old. But he may be used for wildfowling, once he is steady, and he has become efficient on dummies. The two sports, so similar for a man, because they are basically sports for a 'loner', are entirely different for a dog. He is not likely to come face to face with a goose, or duck, when stalking deer with his master!

On the whole it is easier to train a deer dog than a game dog and it is mostly common sense. But, surprisingly, some dogs do not become keen on deer. My great goose dog, Bear, and later, Honey, never showed any interest in deer, nor would they follow a blood line. Drex, whose sport was confined to pigeons and geese, when he winded his first doe, was convinced that it must be high up in the branches of an oak tree!

On the other hand Butty started late in life, after her father Mole retired, and she took to stalking deer, and finding a dead one, as if I had trained her from the start!

One thing is certain. Any stalker who has a good deer dog will find his pleasure in stalking immensely greater than stalking without a dog, and he will find that he can cover the ground more quickly, because the dog will indicate if there is no deer upwind. It is also easy to work across the wind, and thereby cover more ground: and after a buck is shot there will be no frustrating delays to search dense cover for it.

'Drex . . . was convinced that it must be high up in the branches of an oak tree'

VIII

PICKING-UP

For people who do not shoot, and for those of us whose age make days out with a gun less frequent, picking-up is one of the great pleasures in the shooting field. That is especially true if one has a young dog which one is training.

Professional pickers-up have good experienced dogs who understand what is required of them. But a young dog can be a real worry – or a great joy.

Let me describe Happy's first day picking-up on one of the best grouse moors in Britain. She had had one day's picking-up ducks and redlegs in Suffolk. But, unfortunately, that was the very worst scenting day that I have ever experienced in my whole life, and Happy, who has a first-class nose, was nonplussed by the lack of scent. Even experienced dogs would stand within a yard of a dead partridge lying on the open stubble, unable to scent it at all.

Happy did find a mallard which no-one knew about in a dense cover crop, and she also brought me a young cock pheasant (released undamaged) from the same area, and I hoped that no-one knew about that, either.

The days on the grouse moor were her first experience of grouse. Indeed she did not even imagine that such a bird existed. She had only seen two heather plants in her life – and those were on my rockery, and they were not even ling heather.

At the first drive I was well back behind No. 3. It is my experience that grouse will drop out, year after year, in approximately the same place at each drive on every moor. Butty, her great grandmother in her nineteenth year, Happy and I, crouched in a hollow at the foot of rising ground, 500 yards behind the butts. How often it is the extra energy required to rise up a slope that causes a wounded bird to drop out. There was a suspicion of drizzle, but nothing dropped out of the packs and coveys that passed over us.

When the drive was over I moved back to hunt the heather behind the butts. A black labrador and a spaniel were hunting bare (burnt) ground, 100 yards behind the line. They found nothing and, when they had finished, I sent Happy out. She raced off like a greyhound for 300 yards and I wondered how many drives later it would be before I met up with her again! But she came tearing back to my whistle. Then she started to work beautifully. She found a few feathers beside a slight hollow, twice as wide as a bath but only half the depth and about as long. She worked like a Hoover around this and then quested into it, and plunged under an overhanging clump of heather. She came out with her First Grouse, a fine old cock. So proud was she that she danced around, showing it to everyone, and not delivering it at once. Well, I was proud too, and overjoyed. She had wiped the eyes of two experienced dogs. Such a moment is a great occasion in the life history of any dog!

At the last drive there was a lot of shooting at my end of the line. But, again, there was a lost bird well out. Happy went far out, working nicely, and found it at once, delivering perfectly. After that she worked beautifully and I knew that the area which she had covered was devoid of birds – and is that not as important for a picker-up as finding a well marked bird?

The third drive was disappointing for my dogs. The guns' dogs picked all their birds except one which I stumbled upon. Happy picked it, but it hardly counted as a lost bird.

The first drive after lunch was a return drive. As it happened, the guns at the far end had most of the shooting. Three birds came to one of the guns in front of me. He shot two to a right and left, then, changing guns, shot the third – an example of nice shooting. His spaniel picked all three birds.

I thought that the next gun shot only one bird, but I saw him pick a brace. The gun beyond also worked his own dogs. I was walking back with Happy, letting her work, when she picked a bird that no one had seen fall, only ten yards behind a butt.

The last drive was a down-wind drive and a lot of birds came. The weather was hellish – driving rain and a strong wind. Visibility was almost completely obscured by the rain on my glasses. But I did pick out a wounded bird in the first pack. It came down 300 yards from me and 500 yards behind the butts. I could only mark the line. After the drive I worked both dogs and they covered all the likely ground, well. Then I cast them another 50 yards downwind and dear old Butty found something of interest, perhaps where a hare had been. Happy rushed to her to investigate, then raced off nose to ground down a grassy area between much heather, for 100

'She came out with her First Grouse'

yards. 'Oh hell,' I muttered, 'she is on a hare.' No-one could see her. At the far end of the grass, she started to work really well, and suddenly a winged grouse fluttered up, and she had it at once, and was back with it in no time – as good a piece of dog work as any first class dog could do, and better than most do.

It was then that I realised that I have a superb little dog, with the makings of one of the best ever. Such moments are precious indeed! How I wish I could give her lots and lots of little outings, as I used to be able to do with most of my earlier dogs.

It had been a pig of a day in driving rain and half a gale, with a bag only half what it should have been in decent weather. But those raindrops will always be pink in my memory and one little yellow lab is wearing a golden halo! Happiness may be said to be a cigar (with which I would not disagree). But it is also the rapport between dog and man, when the dog has been outstanding. Happy in name and deed!

The following day was lovely hot sun. Both dogs retrieved well. But Happy found a number (3 brace) of 'cemetery grouse' – fruity corpses unpicked from previous days.

The next day we were kept off the moor all day by low cloud and fog. Of course that was the day when I had been invited to carry a gun.

Thursday proved to be a wonderful day. I saw more grouse than I have ever seen before. At one stage a pack of some 1500 broke out of the drive, but the guns in the butts were still shooting hard. Butty disgraced herself and ran in after grouse that came low over our heads. But she came back with a bird. Perhaps she had been watching it all the time.

Happy did well, but failed on one bird. However she made a marvellous retrieve at a towered bird that I had marked. She went back 200 yards for it.

The last day was delayed by fog which took some time to lift. There was time for only four drives, but grouse were in fantastic numbers. At the last drive I estimated 3000 grouse came past me. 64½ brace were picked at this drive. Happy worked well all day and did some very good retrieves. She knows what it is all about and she has become a good grouse dog.

Here is a good picking-up story. A picker-up was using a young black labrador. At lunchtime this dog kept wandering off, so the picker-up went after his dog who, by then, had reached the keeper. Feeling embarrassed, he stooped down, picked up the dog and started to carry it back, as a punishment. The keeper's voice came to him: 'Hey, what are you doing with *my* dog?'

I knew a lady picker-up in East Anglia, who had excellent labradors for the job. She told me that at one shoot a cock pheasant came past her and she put up her shooting stick at it as if she held a gun. The bird fell dead! I remember that BB told me a similar story. He was following hounds on foot when a hen pheasant rose and came back over him. He mounted his stick and the bird fell, but I believe that on this occasion it had swerved into a branch. Anyway, he picked it.

I can relate two other instances of pheasants falling without a shot. In Ross-shire, a hanging cover was being driven from north to south. The wood was just under a long ridge over which was blowing a very severe westerly gale. Two cock pheasants, at different periods during the drive, were flying south just in the shelter of the trees. When they flew beyond the last tree the full force of the gale hit them and twisted their right wing over their back breaking it at the shoulder. Both cocks were picked by the pickers-up, who related this extraordinary event to me.

An amateur picker-up, with a young dog, must give way to the professionals, who know exactly where to stand at each drive. It is essential that the guns should know exactly where the pickers-up are placed.

For a young dog, picking-up pheasants, total obedience is essential. So often there are many pheasants on the ground and the dog has to learn to take no notice of them and to hunt a wounded bird only. A picker-up who puts out half the birds from the next drive is not popular! But a sensible dog soon learns to follow a blood scent.

What pleasure there is when one's young dog finds a bird that others have been unable to locate.

One important thing for a picker-up at a shoot where he does not know the form, is to ascertain where the next drive is to take place, and how he is expected to get there. Sometimes a picker-up may have to go for a very distant bird, and occasionally this may necessitate missing the next drive. But if his dog succeeds, he will be a happy man. He must also become efficient at putting down a live bird quickly, and humanely.

Picking-up at a duck shoot is excellent practice for a young dog, especially if the duck are falling into water. By the end of the drive, or flight, a wounded duck may have travelled a long way and a wounded duck (or goose) is adept at tucking itself away. Luckily they leave a strong scent.

Every wildfowler knows that a winged duck, falling on land, will make for water. But one that falls on water will make for the bank, if there is no man there waving his arms and shouting! When it is safe, a swimming duck or goose should be given a second shot to finish it. Aim at the head, which is usually held flat on the water.

When I first started shooting, I was told that if I shot at a sitting pigeon, or crow, I should aim at its feet. So a shot at a swimming duck's head should be aimed just short of it, unless the bird is a long way out. For all that, swimming ducks (or sitting pigeons!) are not always easy to kill!

When picking up game with a young dog, often there are unruly dogs present. Nothing is worse for a young dog than to see another dog run in, especially at a bird which your dog has marked as his.

At a shoot where some of the guns have their own dogs, it is polite to ask that gun if he wishes to use his dog. It is annoying when a picker-up picks all the birds one has shot, when one wanted experience for one's own dog. It is worse still when someone's dog collects and runs off with the birds one has left at one's peg.

The game cart (or Land Rover) is an important part of any shoot. The picker-up should hand the game he has collected to the man in charge, who should have binder twine already cut to a suitable length with which to hang the game, young being kept separate from old. Any birds which are badly shot should be hung separately.

At every shoot there is nearly always an observant gun who has carefully marked a wounded bird. But every picker-up soon gets to assess the man who has imaginary wounded birds scattered all over the countryside. Usually he has few, if any, dead birds near his peg.

There is the story of the well-dressed young man who took his place as outside gun beside a road. He shot brilliantly and after the drive his labrador had picked all his birds in no time at all. Carrying his birds he bundled his dog and gun and the birds into his car — and drove off, never to be seen again!

Wounded birds fall in strange places. At a grouse drive I shot at the last grouse of the drive, behind the line. It was wounded and I had plenty of time to watch it. It fell dead by the running board of my host's vehicle at the lunch hut. Another time I put a hen pheasant through the window of my host's Range Rover. Luckily the window was open.

I have seen a towered partridge fall against the window of a cottage some distance away. The bird was lying on the doorstep amongst much broken glass, when picked. A few seasons ago at a pheasant shoot a tall pigeon fell onto the floor of a passing lorry. The driver would be surprised when he reached his destination and, no doubt, would have preferred a pheasant.

Often birds stick up in a bush or tree. Frequently a good dog will indicate this, because he can wind small drops of blood which have fallen to the ground. Most shooting men have seen a bird fall through a greenhouse or conservatory. To some extent this has been caused by the host placing a gun where this is an obvious risk.

I have seen a goose fall dead in a field used for pigs. The goose was demolished by a group of hungry Large Whites before any dog could reach it. At the same shot, a goose hit at morning flight, fell among the vehicles parked a long way away, and lay on its back on the green grass — a gift from heaven as no-one knew that it had been wounded.

Birds that hit a human being can cause nasty injuries. A shot pheasant will knock a man to the ground. A tall greylag that I shot fell on a fellow gun. He was flattened into the marsh, but, by amazing good fortune, he was not seriously injured.

When accompanied by a young dog, I shot a pigeon which fell on the dog's head. When I sent him for other pigeons that evening, he would not bring them to hand, but stuffed them down rabbit holes, where he reckoned that they could not attack him again.

On one occasion, when shooting in Anglesey, I shot a teal coming down wind, high, on a full scale gale. The teal fell over a stone wall, where my companion was working his spaniel. By an amazing coincidence, the teal

66

fell on the head of the spaniel. That dog refused to pick anything for the rest of the day!

At a grouse drive in Wales, one butt was on top of a small knoll. Three grouse came to the gun in that butt. He shot one with his first barrel, missed the second, and the third flew into his empty gun. He was covered in blood and feathers and he has always regretted that he had not killed a right and left, thus wiping out all three.

How often one sees the bag thrown into the back of a Land Rover, all muddy and bloody, with the dogs piling in together on top. That is a disgrace! All game should be treated with respect and hung as quickly as possible. Worse still is to leave dogs and game together in a vehicle. Often a dog may start to lick a speck of blood. It is a small step between doing that, and eating the whole bird! The dog is hardly to blame for that and ever after may be hard mouthed.

A dog that runs in is an abomination. A gun that does so is worse!

'By an amazing coincidence, the teal fell on the head of a spaniel'

IX

DOGS IN LITERATURE

He was a gash an' faithfu' tyke,
As ever lap a sheugh or dyke.
His honest, sonsie baws'nt face
Ay gat him friends in ilka place . . .
                    Robert Burns, *Twa dogs*

One of the best known and saddest of all dog stories concerns Gelert in Wales. This favourite and faithful dog was left in charge of the baby, when master and his wife had to go out for the day. When the man returned, the crib was turned over and the baby was lying on the floor in a pool of blood. The man was so incensed that he drew his sword and slew the dog, who still had blood on his muzzle. Then, behind an upturned chair, he saw the body of a wolf, which his dog had killed after a terrible battle. The baby was unharmed and the blood had come from the wolf.

Let this sad story be a lesson to all would-be dog trainers, whose temper is short. Never chastise a dog unless you are certain that he has done wrong, and that the dog understands this equally well.

The village where the event related above took place is still called Beth-gelert – the grave of Gelert. It is one of the wettest areas in Great Britain where an annual rainfall of 100 inches has been recorded. For this reason Bethgelert is no place for game, except for an odd woodcock in winter. But I have a true local shooting story: a forester, who lived in Bethgelert, was given a pair of young homing pigeons. In due course these two pigeons had grown strong enough to be allowed to fly, and the forester opened the door of the loft. He stood outside his house full of the pride of all pigeon fanciers as he watched his pigeons circling high above the house. Suddenly he became aware of a speck in the sky above the two pigeons. Like a winged arrow a peregrine, coming from Snowdon, stooped, and took one of his

'. . . dogs have helped the shooting man for generations'

pigeons. The forester, full of natural anger, rushed into his house for his gun. 'The b–y peregrine won't get the other,' he muttered, as he raised the gun – and shot the surviving pigeon! Though unfortunate for the pigeon, this was lucky for the forester as shooting peregrines is against the law.

Because Scotland is a land of great sport, dogs have helped the shooting man for generations of good shooting. Today, dogs have become famous for rescuing lost hill walkers, but I believe St Bernards carrying a nip of brandy are not used. No doubt, if they were, the numbers lost on the hill would increase!

That very great sportsman, naturalist and splendid author, Charles St John, was a great dog man. He had deerhounds, bird dogs (pointers and setters), a bloodhound, a Newfoundland, a Russian poodle and a bulldog. He reckoned that his bulldog was the best dog for a wounded deer. That dog would follow the line, finish the wounded deer, and then return to his master and lead him back to the dead deer. But he recommends a Skye terrier as the best breed for roe stalking.

On the famous occasion when he shot the Muckle Hart of Benmore, he was alone, having left Bran, his deerhound, with a friend, and, when he found the footprints of the great hart at dusk, he slept out in the heather, so as to follow up the deer at first light, having fed on a grouse that he had shot and cooked. (He and the friend and Bran had slept the previous night in an illicit still, and the friend was in no condition to continue the next day!)

Unfortunately he wounded the hart and without his famous dog, he had difficulty in finishing the animal. Indeed when he approached it, it actually attacked him, and damaged his leg. Incidentally in those far off days a shootable stag was classed as a 'hart' before it was assessed as shootable: a term of venery which is no longer used.

He has many tales to tell of the sagacity of his dogs and of the exploits of some of his shepherd friends' dogs, in *Wild Sports and Natural History of the Highlands*. This book and his *A Scottish Naturalist* are full of observations on natural history of immense interest and value to modern day naturalists. It is surprising that so many observations could be made by one man, so long ago.

With much fine sport available in Scotland, tales of the exploits of many different breeds of dogs are legion. Dogs have helped sportsmen to succeed with such a variety of quarry from red deer to geese and snipe.

On a stormy and windy day in the third week of October in one locality, Charles St John shot 6 grouse, 13 partridge, 1 woodcock, 1 pheasant, 1 mallard, 4 snipe, 2 Jack snipe, 1 teal, 3 curlew, 4 golden plover, 5 hares and 2 rabbits during a walk of a few hours. What a mixed bag! That was because he had promised to send a hamper of game to a friend in Edinburgh! He was accompanied by a single pointer and an old retriever. What sportsman, today, could achieve such a bag, even excluding the two species now protected? He rightly preferred such a day to a much greater bag of 50 or 70 brace of grouse. On this wonderful day he saw also roebuck and blackcock.

That other fantastic sportsman/naturalist of long ago, J.G. Millais, in *The Wildfowler in Scotland* tells of his fine wildfowling bitch, Jet. Once, in a very turbulent sea, a huge wave stunned her and he had to plunge in himself to rescue her. On another time whilst on the Tay, he wing-tipped a Brent goose. The bitch followed the goose into the current of a very high spring tide and they were carried down beyond the point of no return. He managed to obtain a boat and recovered dog and goose; but it took him four hours to return to safety against the current!

From the age of eleven Millais would set out from Dunbar, armed with an eight-bore, and walk the whole length of the east coast of Scotland, from Dunbar to near Thurso, leaving out only the cliffs. This he did on three occasions, sending his bag on ahead, covering fifteen to twenty miles a day, often not going to bed at all. What a wonderful introduction to wildfowling and natural history! Is there a man today (let alone a young lad) who could do the same? 'Days of perfect freedom when Time goes by as shadows on the grass.' No wonder that he became one of the greatest.

The story of *The Hound of the Baskervilles* is immortalised by Conan Doyle in one of the Sherlock Holmes adventures. Another famous dog in literature is *Jock of the Bushvelt*. That old book held me entranced as a young lad. Jim Corbett's Robin was a dog that accompanied him on many an adventure in the jungles of India, as mentioned in his famous *Man Eaters of Kumaon*. Frank Wallace, the great deer stalker and artist, relates the story of his dog Jock in his book *Happier Years*. Alas the dog had a sad end to his short life.

Let me list some of the best books written about dogs for dog owners. That great dog man Richard Sharpe wrote *Gundog Training by Amateurs*, a book full of expert advice. Peter Moxon, who for very many years wrote about dogs, weekly, in the *Shooting Times*, wrote *Gundogs – Training and Field Trials* and also *Gundogs – Questions and Answers*. His expertise is outstanding. All one needs to know about springer spaniels will be found in D.M. Hooper's book *The Springer Spaniel* and Talbot Radcliffe, who used to breed and train Welsh springers and export some to America, wrote *Spaniels for Sport*, a useful book.

Veronica Heath, another regular contributor to sporting magazines, who lives in Northumberland, wrote *A Dog at Heel*, especially useful for picking-up and beaters' dogs. Michael Brander has contributed *The Rough Shooter's Dog* and *Training the Pointer Retriever Gundog*. One of the greatest breeders of labradors was the Countess Lorna Howe. Together with G. Waring she wrote a most useful book *The Labrador Retriever*. Another invaluable guide is *Retriever Training* by S. Scales.

Two handbooks cover GSPs and Weimeraners. The GSP handbook from the USA, *German Shorthaired Pointers* is most useful: and the *Weimeraner Handbook* is also of USA origin.

A little known book is Joe Irving's *Gundogs, Their Learning Chain* and Tony Jackson, one time editor of the *Shooting Times*, edited *Hunter Pointer Retriever* which covers the HPR breeds, written by different authors.

Keith Erlandson, well-known author of shooting magazine articles, wrote *Gundog Training* which emphasises Field Trial training and contains a great deal of sound advice; *Working Gundogs* by Martin Deeley is another very useful book.

A book by two vets, J. Bower and G. Waring, *The Health of your Dog* is an excellent guide to caring for and breeding dogs.

There are of course many other good books and for pleasant reading Town Gun's *The Worst Dog in the World* is outstanding.

However for the raw beginner, *The Complete Gundog* compiled by John

Humphreys which includes chapters for each breed by specialist authors, is outstanding value.

Finally, a delightful book by Chapman Pincher *One dog and her man* is an excellent read, and should be in every dog lover's bookcase.

'*. . . by setting publication back by some days*'

POEMS

DREX

(With apologies to Elizabeth Barrett Browning)

What was he doing, the great dog Drex,
Down in the reeds by the river?
He wanted to please and not to vex
As he splashed in the reeds by the river.
'Twas a wounded goose he'd seen come down –
Down in the reeds by the river.
So he dashed away, and crossed the bog,
(As strong as an ox, this great big dog,
As he hunted the reeds by the river.)
With a honking cry the goose flapped out –
'Hi-lost, he's there!' his Master did shout
As the goose swam away down the river.
And now undeterred, Drex swam behind,
The goose would be his, his own good find
As they swam far away down the river.
Ten minutes later, covered in mud,
He appeared from the reeds by the river.
In his big mouth was a great wild goose
He'd retrieved from the reeds by the river!

November 1982

TEAL

(*A Friend's Dog*)

Warm brown eyes and a heart of gold:
One forgot that, one day, you'd grow old.
Black as night and much too fat –
You were never any worse for that!
All day you'd hunt, on hill or shore –
No other dog could e'er do more:
Ptarmigan, goose, woodcock or grouse:
A lovely companion in the house.
Always happy as the day is long,
But, out with a gun was where you'd belong!
And in between, nice pups you bred
(Once, long ago, to my Bear you were wed!)
And now, I hear, with a heavy heart,
That Robin and you have had to part.
Never again, with a waving tail
Will we follow a winged cock pheasant's trail.
Tales of your exploits will always be told
As the pages of memory slowly unfold
And, when its my turn for 'the end of the lane'
We'll flight celestial wildfowl again!
For I think that somehow you always knew
That, in my quiet way, I loved you too.

March 1983

JAMIE

When first we met, your youth had passed:
No longer could you run so fast:
You had the most endearing ways,
Such squeals of joy: welcome displays!
Often you'd bring a little stone –
Present it like a tasty bone!

Alas, later, your health got low:
You tried never to let it show.
Slowly your strength began to fail –
And yet you always wagged your tail.
But, now, dear Jamie, you have gone.
No more we'll hear your happy song.

Even the daisies on the lawn
Feel all unfertilised, forlorn!
Come sun or rain, by night or day
Sweet memory will with us stay.
For, always, we'll remember you
Happy, loyal and always true.

BUTTY

We stalked the forests and shot the moor,
And shared many a wonderful hour on the shore.
Mother of many, most of them best,
You lived your life with consistent zest:
Fearless in gorse or prickly thorn,
You treated hazards with canine scorn!
You were always best at geese and grouse.
When alone, you'd steal my chair in the house.
There's now such a space beside that chair:
So often you seem still to be there!

You'd carry a Canada, and wind a roe:
And chase every hare – if I'd let you go!
Now, you have gone: your great heart still.
No longer I'll see your brown eyes thrill
When I take my gun from its safe place:
That's when your pulse would really race!
So patient with Happy, the boisterous one,
Whose sporting life has just begun!
Butty, old pal, I salute you for aye:
I shall remember you – 'til I die.

May 1992

'Whispering wings . . .'

MORNING FLIGHT

Hard to rise – alarm bell ringing!
Stumble down and get the gun.
Two brown eyes, with tail a swinging:
Jump in the car – our day's begun.

The tang of saltings stirs our heartbeats
As I park, clear of the gate.
Dog and man share expectation.
No-one else, and we're not late.

We're there at last, out on the foreshore
Squelching through the plocking mud,
All around still dark and chill raw,
Slimey from the night tide's flood.

Crouching in a sticky gutter
Waiting for the duck to flight.
Whispering wings: hen wigeon stutter:
To the east the first new light.

Bottle shapes across the skyline
Far away the curlew cry:
Mallard making for the tide line –
Hold your fire, they are too high.

From a sandbank pinkfeet clamour:
Magic! Will they come my way?
They're up! Crouch low, down in your gutter:
They pass too wide! No shot today.

Use your fieldglass – are those greylag?
Watch the 'fowl as the tide mounts.
What 'fowler minds an empty gamebag?
'Tis 'Hope' and 'Being There' that counts!